A Rainbow Book

PEOPLE
IN
PIECES:

MULTIPLE PERSONALITY
IN
MILDER FORMS
&
GREATER NUMBERS

❖

ALAN MARSHALL, Ph.D.

❖

RAINBOW BOOKS, INC.

PEOPLE IN PIECES:
Multiple Personality In Milder Forms & Greater Numbers
by Alan Marshall, Ph.D.
Cover Design by David Helwer
Interior Design by Marilyn Ratzlaff
$12.95
ISBN: 0-935834-94-X

Library of Congress Cataloging-in-Publication Data
Marshall, Alan, 1941-
    People in pieces : multiple personality in milder forms & greater numbers / Alan Marshall.
        p.   cm.
    Includes bibliographical references.
    ISBN 0-935834-94-X : $12.95
    1. Multiple personality. I. Title
RC569.5.M8M37   1993
616.85'236 — dc20   92-32414
                                                              CIP

Recognizing the importance of preserving the written word, Rainbow Books, Inc., by policy, prints all of its first editions on acid-free (neutral pH) paper.

CONTENTS

FOREWORD

Jacques Cousteau is a lucky man. He gets to dive to depths of the sea where he can witness a very different and fascinating world. Psychotherapists are lucky also. The world they work in is quite different from the usual workaday world. They are permitted access to a realm of human experience that lies beyond routine awareness. They are invited to accompany people into the domain of the Unconscious, and they are paid to be guides in that strange and forbidding territory.

For both Cousteau and psychotherapists, there is an implied responsibility. If in their explorations they stumble onto something noteworthy, they are expected to report it. And to do so with as much candor and accuracy as possible. Even if the subject matter is not entirely new, they may witness it at a different depth or from another perspective. And when seen in that particular way, it may prove helpful or enlightening in some regard.

That's how this book came into being. I have been engaged and fascinated by the subject matter for over six years. My written account of it is what scientists call a Hypothetical Model. A Model does not claim to be "The Truth." Rather it is simply one way of looking at the phenomenon that provides for some degree of elucidation and suggests a path for further inquiry. To whatever extent this Model fits with and sheds helpful light on the subject, it is of value. I have no doubt that it will in its turn be replaced by something more illuminating. If the present work provides a means to that improvement, it will be worth it.

CHAPTER I

"SALLY"

Sally's daddy is screaming at her. He does it a lot. She can never seem to figure out what it was she did that was so awful. The shouting is hurting her head real bad and the tears are burning her eyes and she wants to run away. But she can't. He's bigger and faster and he would catch her and make it a lot worse. Just when she can't endure another moment of this, a magical thing happens. She disappears. Not physically, but mentally. Her body is still there just like before, except that there is a vacant look in her eyes. Because her mind is elsewhere. Just when her little heart was about to break, her brain tripped a switch, and she found herself sitting in her grandma's lap eating freshly-baked brownies. All warm and cuddly, she gestures to her puppy to jump up and join them. She stays there until she gets a signal that it is reasonably safe to go back home.

I want to propose three different ways that this story could develop. First, it could turn out okay, and Sally would grow up to be essentially normal. Second, things could get terribly bad; she could experience severe abuse and develop Multiple Personality Disorder. Or third, it might turn out somewhere in between. In that case, she could develop something I'll call Ego State Disorder, which is what this book is about. Since you've probably never heard of that (it doesn't officially exist yet as a diagnostic category), I'll describe it by contrasting it with the other two scenarios.

NORMAL SALLY

Let's say her dad only screams at her occasionally. And the rest of her life is pretty good. Her mom loves her, almost as much as her grandma, and her dad is just moody. She'll probably be fine. Sure, there will be some times when things will get real bad, and her brain may have to trip this same switch again. But not too often. And it might even come in handy. If she has to sit in a dentist's chair for a couple of hours having a difficult root canal, she will be glad to have this merciful capacity to "go somewhere else" in her mind.

Sally will not be precisely the same person all the time. Certainly she will behave differently at church than at a raucous birthday party. And she too will have varying moods, like her father. Sometimes she will care for him deeply, and at other times despise him (say, during adolescence). But basically she will be one person, despite the variability in moods and attitudes. She will have a simple, uncomplicated sense of who she is and what she likes and doesn't like. And she will probably remember a few key events from almost every year of her life after age three or four.

SALLY AS A
MULTIPLE PERSONALITY

Now to the opposite end of the continuum, to Multiple Personality. To get here, Sally's life will have to be much worse. There will be a great likelihood that the abuse will be not only emotional, but probably sexual as well. It will occur fairly often, most likely at the hands of an adult. (Molestation by a sibling or another youngster is not usually as traumatic unless done in a way that causes great physical pain.) It is possible that there will be someone in her life who will love her, but even that will be tainted by the fact that this person is unable or unwilling (in Sally's mind) to protect her from the horror of the sexual abuse. Each time it occurs, her brain will throw the exit switch, and she will be thrust into the world of fantasy.

Imagine, if you will, what happens to her then. After the adult is finished with her (I know how crude that sounds, but that is how the child perceives it), she has to somehow come back to reality. What is she supposed to do for the rest of the day? How is she going to make herself keep her mouth shut? (The abuser made sure she understood that it would kill her mother if she found out!) What about her rage? What about the physical pain? She can scarcely walk — how is she to conceal that? Part of her wants to die. Part of her wants to kill. Ten different emotions and voices rage in her head.

Then suddenly all is quiet. She doesn't look exactly like the Sally we knew before; the smile is waxy, and the movements are stiff. But she manages to put one foot in front of the other. She gets to the bathroom and scrubs herself everywhere she can reach. She feels a little better. She puts her clothes on. After a while, she goes outside to play.

What has happened? How did it get so quiet all of a sudden?

Because an Alter was formed and took control. An Alter is a new personality segment that is created to deal with some sort of extreme trauma. Rather than try to explain this, I'll describe the actual process. This particular Alter — we'll call it Josie — knew what had to be done. The situation called for mental toughness. All the other voices and feelings had to be made to shut up. If they kept on with their agonizing, someone out there in the world was soon going to start asking questions, and that would finish her, as well as her mother.

She had to concoct some sort of smile that looked believable and to pretend that everything was fine. There was no choice. She had to make her body real numb in order to pull this off, and so she did it. There had been that little voice crying about the pain, and it wasn't going to quit, so she knocked it for a loop. So too for the others — the rage and the humiliation and all the rest. She managed to stuff them into the icebox so they would hush and let her go on living. By now there was no zest in her life, nor any peace.

But she was breathing, and at that moment that was the best she could do.

But Josie wasn't nuclear-powered. Sometimes she got tired. Those other brats just wouldn't quit — they were constantly pushing to come out. They seemed determined to let Sally in on what happened all those times after she drifted away into fantasyland and get her to do something about it. Keeping them in the freezer was a lot of work. Especially at night. They could get loose then and start telling stuff in Sally's dreams. They soon discovered that they couldn't be TOO direct about what happened, because she would wake up screaming, and that would be the end of that. So they soon learned to just show her small pieces of the puzzle, hoping that maybe one day she could put them all together. One night it might be part of the pain she felt way up in her tummy, and then on a different night something about the color of the rug where it usually happened.

Pretty soon "Sally" was just a shell. Josie was in charge nearly all the time. People still called her "Sally," but Josie knew *she* was the real power behind the throne. Still, there was continual unrest on the inside. Josie was most afraid of the one she called Tattletale. As Sally grew older, she found a peculiar pleasure in telling on the other kids in school. She had no idea why, and it got her in a lot of trouble, but she seemed compelled to do it. Somehow "telling on somebody" made her feel better.

For her own part, Josie insisted on perfect behavior because that way nobody became suspicious. That damned Tattletale was flirting with disaster. Occasionally Josie would have to bash her a good one, causing an intense headache which seemed to Sally to come out of nowhere. There were many times that Josie wished she could just kill off all the others. Silence them permanently so she could get a little rest. She was convinced that ending their lives would have no effect at all upon her own. The sense of separation became so complete that she was sure she would survive even though they were actually, physically dead.

One of the things that Josie dreaded the most was

when she would get caught napping during the day and one of the others seized control for a while. Sally would be completely unable to tolerate their presence, and so she would do her disappearing act. She would then have amnesia for the entire time that Alter was in control. One time she "awakened" out of an amnestic state to find all the soap used in her bathroom and the towels soaking wet. Someone unknown to her had apparently been scrubbing itself very clean. Josie would finally prevail of course, after a pitched battle, and force them back into the freezer. Sally would feel exhausted, as though she had been fighting for her life.

Another one of the Alters was called the Wimp because it cried all the time. The tears were from shame. Like all the others, it managed to get out now and then. Sometimes, in later years, Sally would find herself crying for no apparent reason. There was a peculiar bittersweet quality about it, too; almost like she was glad to find out that she still could form tears. It seemed to remind her of being alive in a way that she usually knew nothing about — kind of like her childhood. She seemed to know almost nothing about that either. She did have a few memories, but there were entire years that seemed to be completely lost to her.

SALLY WITH EGO STATE DISORDER

Now for the middle ground. In this case, Sally might well still be sexually abused, but less often, and perhaps by someone she didn't know — possibly by a distant uncle who only visited occasionally. He would still make sure she didn't tell, and it would be very traumatic, but not as bad as if it were a parent or a loved one. And the abuse wouldn't necessarily have to be of a sexual nature. It could be constant humiliation or physical beating. But overall, there would probably be more love and nurturing in her life than had she turned out to be a Multiple. There would not be as many periods of amnesia either, and they would be of shorter duration. There would not be the huge gaps in memory that there would be for a Multiple, but she would still notice a big difference between her recall and that of most of her friends.

She would most likely be indecisive. She would often not know how to decide something because she didn't really know how she felt about it. It would bother her that she would be more changeable than most people. She would vacillate between feeling one way at one moment and then quite differently at another. Her friends would think she was fickle and rather untrustworthy. In general, she would notice that she *had* fewer feelings than most people. The ones she had would seem more superficial and fleeting. There would also be a gnawing sense of incompleteness and only a dim awareness of what it might be like to be whole. Like a Multiple, she would have a number of separate personality Parts, called Ego States. The number would be much smaller, say from three to six, whereas Multiples often have twenty or thirty Alters.

She might well live out her entire life this way and have no clear indication that there was ever anything wrong. After all, she had friends, and she could keep a job and manage a family life; but barely, and without really enjoying much of it.

There are several ways that she might accidentally get shaken out of her stupor. One would be for her stress level to get out of control. When the controlling and repressing Ego State (similar to Josie, above) gets overwhelmed, the other Parts grab the chance and make their move. All hell can break loose. They typically try to show too much too fast, with the result that Sally feels on the edge of a nervous breakdown. Certain drugs could do it also, especially hallucinogenic drugs. These can compromise the mind's usual ways of defending itself, with the same resulting upsurgence of the repressed Parts.

Or, something in Sally's current life might remind her forcefully of her past. For example, when her daughter gets to be close to the age at which her own abuse occurred, she might catch a particular look in her eye, or some little gesture, that would catapult her back suddenly into her own childhood. The memories might or might not actually return at that point. But there would be a lot of anxiety, trembling, and feelings of impending doom. She would then have to find a way to either repress it all the more firmly or do something to get it out.

CHAPTER II

EGO STATE DISORDER

The reason for providing this background is to set the stage for describing Ego State Disorder. I'm betting there are at least ten million Americans who are afflicted by it. Currently, the closest we come to diagnosing it is in a wastebasket category called "Atypical Dissociative Disorder."* I think we can do better than that. But in order to make sense of ESD, we need more information about Multiple Personality Disorder (MPD).

DISSOCIATION AS THE BASIS FOR MPD

Think back to Sally. The magical switch that transported her from unbearable reality into pleasant fantasy is a process we call Dissociation. It means exactly what it sounds like. When the pain gets too bad, we *dis*-associate ourselves from it in order to go on living. In Sally's case, she fled to her grandma's lap. In her Multiple Personality scenario, I said that the abuse would have been repeated many

---

*There are proposals to add three new categories to the Dissociative Disorders section of the *Diagnostic and Statistical Manual (DSM-IV)*, but none of them are close in nature to Ego State Disorder.

times. So too the dissociation. I also said that she had to form an Alter (Josie), a new personality segment, in order to become tough enough to survive.

Now exactly where did this Alter come from? Sally was not suddenly inhabited by demons, nor did she make something up out of thin air. She had been a basically nice, compliant child. But she had passed the age of two, and so she certainly knew how to say NO with gusto and had seen plenty of examples of people acting tough on TV and at home. Undoubtedly, she too had given it a whirl. So the potential was there. She had never *had* to act tough for any length of time before, but she knew how to do it when it was required. Josie was thus the coalescence of all these capacities and experiences into one personality element.

I also said Josie made the others "shut up," that she could "knock them for a loop," and "put them into the freezer." Obviously these are just metaphors. The "freezer" is of course the Unconscious (although many psychologists would argue that I'm just trading one metaphor for another). Unfortunately, we don't yet have a means of empirically accounting for how these processes occur and no clear consensus as to whether they occur at all. There is simply no way at present to prove much of this scientifically.

So I'm going to ask you, the reader, to temporarily suspend your rational, analytic mode. What I want to engage is your *intuition*. If what you read makes sense to that part of you, I'll be satisfied. We are going to wander in some strange territory, and our conventional road maps will be of limited use. After almost six years of witnessing the same phenomena that we will encounter, it is still sometimes surprising to me. So I can well understand if you are skeptical. (My own rational side is from Missouri.)

MORE ABOUT ALTERS

Let's just assume for the moment that Josie really can make the others shut up, go to the freezer, etc. How come "others" is plural? First, there's really just Sally, and then there's Josie, and now they've suddenly blossomed into Others? Okay. Remember I said that there were a bunch of voices and feelings careening around after the abuse? The feelings were things like pain and humiliation that were demanding to be paid attention to because they needed fixing. The voices were all the conflicting thoughts going on inside her head. One was telling her that of course she would have to report this horror to her mother. Another was insisting that she can't because her mother will die from it. And so too for all the conflicting feelings, perceptions, and attitudes.

These various conflicting elements gradually form the basis for Alters. They become truly separate personalities. I'll try to describe as much of it as I can.

After the abuse, Sally was still a human child. As such, she was much more than just a tough little Alter named Josie. She still had many of the emotional capacities of any other child, even though some were now buried. She could still feel degrees of love, kindness, jealousy, lust, anger, and greed — essentially like any normal person.

But as she grew older, and the abuse continued, she became increasingly fractured. Some part of her would remember all the physical pain of the abuse. This part would hate her father. In order to preserve these feelings and memories, it would have to isolate itself from the opposing parts of her — the ones that loved him. And if the conflict between these parts intensified, both of them would have to be repressed either partially or completely. It is apparently impossible to store recollections of intense pain in the same part of our brain that preserves the love for the very person who caused the pain.

Multiple Personalities usually include a number of Alters that are quite young, who will tell you they never made it to school. When they come out in hypnosis, they want to color or play with blocks or sit on your lap and have you read to them. Each will go by a different name. Some will be male and some will be female. "Jimmy" might be one who recalls mostly the rage at being abused, as well as the physical pain. It will be natural for him to be male, since his memories impel him toward beating up his tormentor. Let's try to trace his development.

"JIMMY"

A while after the molestations, Sally would go into what her mother thought were temper tantrums. She would turn blue and would beat her head on the floor until it knocked her senseless. Afterward, she would go back to being her usual compliant self, and her mother would hope that she had seen the last of these fits. Her mom had no way of knowing that it wasn't a bad temper that was causing these outbursts, but rather one of the internal voices trying to scream out for help. "Mommy! Listen to me! Something is wrong, and I can't tell you! Can't you see from the banging that something is wrong? Don't you know what he did to me? I hate him and I want to kill him!"

With all the clamor going on inside poor Sally's head, Josie certainly has to take control. She cleverly uses Sally's desperate actions against her. She assists her banging her head, and soon enough there is blessed unconsciousness. She has managed to get her back under control. But later on the rage comes out again. And again.

As she grows older, a number of factors converge to make Sally want to stop the fits. For one thing, they hurt like hell, and the headaches last for days. For another, they aren't accomplishing anything. Mom is worried sick and is just not getting the message at all. Lastly, everywhere Sally turns, she sees that people take a dim view of little girls being very angry. So it has to end.

Somehow she manages to stop it. Later, she is vaguely aware that things are more peaceful inside, and she is glad that she stopped it. Mom looks better, too, and is proud of the way Sally is gaining in self-control. So then why does Sally feel late in the night that she has lost a close friend? She doesn't know why and has no stomach for pursuing it.

Once she stops the fits completely, it may be that she

never again finds an outlet for her rage. In that case, these feelings will remain in the background, and the associated memories will remain with them, frozen in place and time. True, they will struggle forward into her dreams, but even there they will have to disguise themselves. Otherwise, it will hit too close to home. Sally will wake up terrified and in a cold sweat, only to be assured by her mother that whatever it was wasn't real and to be a good girl now and let them all get some sleep.

The friend she has lost is Jimmy, the code name for her rage and all the memories associated with it. Jimmy is now a full-blown Alter. Why does it feel like he was a friend? Because he was a vitally important part of her memory and her emotional life. Once he is banished, she loses contact with him. The banishment takes a little while to be finalized, and during this period, there is a dull but persistent feeling that part of herself has died.

True, he contained a lot of ugliness and pain; but without those memories, how is Sally to make any sense out of her life and her behavior? Why is she going to occasionally want to bang her head? How is she to understand her adult tendency to choose men who treat her like dirt? Why doesn't she have a normal sexual appetite? Why does anger scare her to death? In time, she is likely to conclude that she is just weird and may as well try to accept it.

Losing a portion of yourself in this way can be compared to a soldier having to give up a leg that has been mutilated by a land mine explosion. No matter how ugly the leg looks, or how bad it feels, you never want it to be actually, totally taken away from you. You want to keep whatever tiny shred of it you can, because it is part of you. Yes, you can learn to do without it, but it is never quite the same. You can function, but not like the you that once was whole.

"LITTLE SALLY"

As a Multiple, Sally is likely to have lots of Alters in addition to Jimmy and Josie. (Some Multiples have as few as two, but these are fairly rare.) There will be an Alter to deal with and provide memory for her intense desire to love her father. No matter that he has used her cruelly for his own sexual needs. He is still her father, and she cannot deny the primal need to love him (call this Alter "Little Sally"). This basic need is much reinforced by the fact that he is in all likelihood nice to her on some occasions. Even the most abusive parents are nice sometimes. She will bend over backward to please him, hoping against hope that she can prove herself worthy of his love.

She will continue this masochistic-looking behavior *until* she reaches a certain point. That is the point at which Josie will see that trying to love her daddy is killing them. Little Sally will reach out to him again and again and lose a quart of blood each time. She will insist that he is a good daddy and that it is her fault — she just needs to be a better daughter. This will greatly increase the amount of internal conflict because some of the other Alters will see that he is a jerk who deserves little other than their hatred. Finally, Josie will face the fact that she must amputate again. Little Sally has to go. Sally will go through the same quiet grieving process again, with the same vague sense that something is dying inside. And soon she will find that there are even more of her feelings and actions that she does not comprehend. And there will be more black holes in her memory bank.

As she gets older, the amputations will continue. A dozen or so Alters will probably be formed and locked away. The resulting personality will look like the chart on the next page.

The outermost layer, Sally, is what the world sees. There is not much to it. It is just a veneer and very fragile, as represented by the thin outer boundary. The next layer, Josie, serves to provide some degree of protection for Sally,

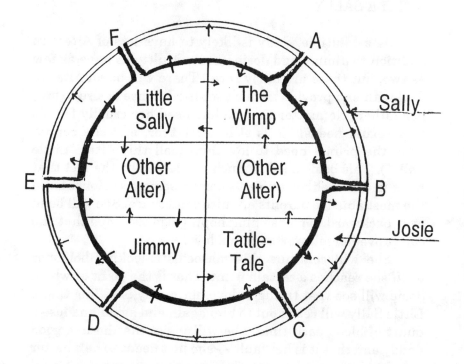

to shield her against intrusions from the outside world. But more importantly, she provides protection from the *inside* world — from all the Alters and all the memories that push incessantly toward Sally's consciousness. Here too, the boundary separating Sally from Josie is quite thin and highly permeable — but only from the inside out, not from the outside in. In other words, Josie has nearly total access to Sally in order to be able to control most of what she does. But the boundary is like a one-way mirror. It is highly *imper*meable from the outside in, meaning that Sally has virtually no awareness that any creature called Josie even exists. The direction of the arrows depicts this one-way access.

I know that many people find this difficult to believe. When Kenneth Bianchi (the Los Angeles "Hillside Strangler") was arrested, he had no idea why. He was dumbfounded, and he wasn't kidding. He had no — zero — awareness of ever doing physical harm to anyone. All he knew was that he blacked out from time to time. It was not until he consented to hypnosis with Dr. John Watkins that it became apparent that there was someone else in there, someone who in fact had killed people. Dr. Watkins (1984) writes:

> "I found Kenneth Bianchi to be a pleasant, mild young man who seemed to be earnestly seeking to understand what had happened and why he was in jail charged with two murders. In describing his childhood, he stated that he had always thought well of his mother ('I would have fought anyone who said anything against her.'), but that he had recently been shown medical records which had brought many doubts to his mind. Reports of his many visits to physicians, school counselors, social workers, and examining psychologists portrayed his mother as having been dominating, overconcerned, trotting him from one clinic to another for his 'nervous' problems (petit mal, allergies, tic, incontinence, many phobias), and refusing to accept psychiatric opinions of an emotional basis for his symptoms. She was also reported to have been both seductive (showing him nude pictures) and cruel (punishing him by holding his hand over a stove burner and beating him with a belt)."

After a number of hypnotic sessions, Kenneth began to have very painful headaches. These proved to be harbingers of the emergence of "Steve," the Alter who did the killing. Finally, Dr. Watkins encouraged Kenneth to try to focus on the headaches and see if he could discern what was causing them. That was when Steve burst forth.

Steve was furious with Dr. Watkins for exposing him. While he remained safely in the background, Steve could do whatever he wanted and not be held accountable. But once his existence was discovered, he would also become known to Kenneth. And that meant trouble. First, because Kenneth would then have to admit to being at least an accessory to the murders. But more importantly, because Steve would be severely limited in carrying out his sociopathic behaviors once Kenneth knew to watch out for him. Even though Steve hated Dr. Watkins, he was delighted to finally have the opportunity to brag about the murders. He eagerly pointed out the pictures in an L.A. paper of which girls he had killed and which ones were killed by his cousin, Angelo Buono.

Unfortunately, the phenomenon is all too real. There is more and more experimental evidence to support the highly diverse nature of the Alters. They individually respond quite differently to electroencephalography (EEG's), for example (Pitblado, 1986). There is also mounting evidence that individual Alters respond quite differently to medications (Putnam, 1989).

Getting back to the diagram, we can next see that the boundary between Josie and the other Alters is thick. This reflects a state in which she has good control over their emergence. You will notice, however, that there are numerous little leakage points (letters A, B, etc.) through which they can gain access to the outside world. Josie has to constantly patrol this boundary to make sure that containment is secure. (I know how metaphorical this is. Again, I can only appeal to your intuition.)

The arrows pointing in both directions — in from Josie to the Alters — and out from the Alters to her — represent the fact that there is mutual awareness, some knowledge of each other in both directions. Among the Alters themselves, the boundaries are of various sorts. Some of the Alters are completely spatially separated, representing the fact that they are totally ignorant of each other's existence. Others may be side by side, and their boundaries may be permeable in both directions. This would be true, for example, between two Alters who shared some of the same basic feelings or memories or attitudes. It would be easy for them to both know about each other and to tolerate the other's presence. Indeed, in some cases, they are even able to provide a measure of support to each other. If the arrows go in one direction only, it suggests that one Alter knows about the adjacent one, but that the knowledge is not mutual. So all manner of combinations is possible and does, in fact, occur.

Incidentally, there is often a significant plus to this disorder: Multiples can be highly skilled in many areas. One can be an excellent writer, another an auto mechanic, and yet a third a fine musician. Admittedly, there is the possibility that the person was born with all these talents, and that this in some way predisposes them to MPD. They also tend to be very bright, and that may be a contributing factor as well.

But one feature comes straight out of the dissociative style of adaptation: *the ability to concentrate exclusively on one thing at a time.* When any given Alter is in control, the others are completely gone. Consider Jimmy. When he is out, he has no regard whatever for social convention nor for any of the things that concern the other Alters. He only knows about anger and ways to express it. Imagine the amount of *focus* that he is capable of! He has the opportunity to develop subtle kinds of awareness having to do with all aspects of anger that most of us would never even know existed, because he can do it without distraction. When most of us would be preoccupied with what to get at the grocery, he is zeroing in on infinitesimal clues that give him a perfect read on someone's level of anger or fear. He could probably be a first-class street fighter, and with a little training in restraint, an exceptional Green Beret.

In a book entitled *Flow,* Csikszentmihalyi (1990) describes those lucky persons who are able to build this ability to focus into their daily lives. They are able to enjoy the pleasures of doing something, whatever it may be, with total involvement. Not surprisingly, that leads to excellence, which is a lot more fun than mediocrity. Many activities are such that, when you reach a higher plateau, you find a whole new array of challenges. Each challenge in turn opens onto a new set of doors. And with each door you pass through, the activity becomes more interesting and absorbing. Multiples may be the best in the world at this. The good news is that if they are successfully treated, these skills essentially stay with them and can serve them well for the rest of their lives. The bad news is that it is one hell of a price to pay.

Having some comprehension of how Multiple Personalities are formed and how they behave sets the stage for the central point of this book: to describe a similar outcome, but one in which the disorder is less severe and less crippling. I believe that it is also much more common and that many readers will see themselves reflected to some degree in the following accounts. (There is a questionnaire at the end of the book that you can fill out to get some idea of whether you personally might fit somewhere in these categories.)

EGO STATE DISORDER (ESD)

Again, Ego States are the counterparts of Alters. They are the Parts into which the personality is divided. But they differ in many ways from Alters:

1. Ego States cannot be elicited except by hypnosis. Alters, on the other hand, can spontaneously seize control of the Multiple's personality without being hypnotically activated.

2. Ego States do not have the same degree of power over the personality as do Alters. They can be elicited and dismissed rather easily whereas Alters are much harder to control.

3. Alters frequently perform acts that are drastically out of keeping with the person's usual behavior. Ego States are less ego-dystonic, meaning that they are usually not so different from the way the person normally behaves and feels.

4. There are usually from three to six Ego States. Alters may number anywhere from two to over a hundred.

5. There is not the same degree of internal conflict among Ego States as there is among Alters. In the former, I have occasionally found one State that fears or hates another so much that it would like to be completely rid of it. But in the case of Alters, one often hears that one is actually plotting to kill another. They sometimes say that they will simply find another material body in which to exist, but the matter is of little concern.

6. When one Alter seizes control, there is usually total amnesia for the primary personality, as well as the other Alters. Thus, the person's memory is like a patchwork quilt, containing many vacancies and much inconsistency. In ESD, the person also may have years of their lives that are without memory. But there are not the recurring blackouts, and there is less overall confusion. There is little or no true amnesia.

7. When Ego States speak, there is often some noticeable difference from the person's usual voice. Even the face may look slightly different, the muscular arrangement altered. In MPD, when a new Alter appears, the differences are usually much more drastic. Vocabulary, voice quality, bodily movements, facial appearance, the manner of laughing — all can be very different. Until a clinician has seen this for himself, it sounds eery and impossible. I think it's like combat; there's no way to *really* understand unless you've been there.

To summarize, Ego State Disorder is a lot like Multiple Personality Disorder, except it is milder. In general, I think that the backgrounds of Multiples are considerably more traumatic than for ESD. I also think the prognosis is better in the case of ESD than MPD. If we were to draw a continuum of Dissociation (the basis for both disorders), it would look like this:

Minimal Dissociation	Moderate Dissociation	Extreme Dissociation
Normal mood changes	Ego State Disorder	Multiple Personality Disorder

One of the things we can see here is that all of these elements are in fact continuous. The "Normal mood changes" category does not have a definite beginning and end point. Rather, it blends in with Ego State Disorder. The latter also blends in with MPD. This helps us to see as well that *within* each category we find a continuum. A person does not "have" ESD. He may have it, but little enough so that he is in fact just on the edge of normal mood changes. Likewise, some cases of MPD are certainly much more severe than others, and some of the least severe would be very hard to demarcate from ESD.

Now, in order to better understand Ego State Disorder, we proceed to a description of it in action, within a psychotherapy setting.

CHAPTER III

"BOB"

We're now going to switch characters. I'm going to try to depict what happened over several years of therapy with three different men, so we need to change genders. I'll roll the group of men into one and call the composite "Bob."

Bob was badly neglected as a child. He was a late arrival after four other sibs, and his mom and dad always felt he was something of an unwanted burden. One early memory was sitting on a small stool, hour after hour, watching his mom cook or clean, always wishing she would take time out to play with him. She rarely did. She was too old and too tired. She was a staunch Catholic, though, and had plenty of energy when it came time to discipline Bob or to put the fear of God in him about sex or some such nasty behavior. She was also quick to taunt and ridicule him — an accepted practice within this particular family line. It was cruelly matriarchal, and most of the women despised and demeaned the men. And Bob had the bad luck to be a young man.

Among the other males that his mother hated was her husband, his father. Having been spurned by her, he of course found solace in the companionship of other women. This gave her consummate justification for loathing him. It also allowed her to enforce a total separation between father and son, for the latter's "own good." So Bob grew up without a dad and with a mother who couldn't stand him.

About the only way he could get any favorable attention from his mom was to talk about how he would grow up and become a priest. Now there was a good boy — not a vulgar, brutish primate like the rest of them, but a potential man of the cloth: sensitive, unselfish, compassionate, and asexual. She could actually like him a little if he sounded really serious about it. But it never lasted long — a day or two at best. Then it was back into the pit.

Bob happened to be a good athlete. Not that anybody in his family cared a lot about it, but he had good athletic genes. And so he learned that he could do a lot of things well that other kids seemed to have to struggle with. He also had a lot of curiosity about how things worked. Since he had so many idle hours, he had plenty of time to take lots of things apart and more or less put them back together. In this way, he learned a lot of fundamental physical principles about the material world. All of this was done basically on his own. No one had the time or patience to show him much.

THE CHILD

From this brief description, we can imagine at least five major personality elements here in embryo. First, there is the very young boy who would do absolutely anything to please his mother, even denying himself almost everything that was true to his nature in order to garner some shred of affection from her. And even when it didn't work, he would try again and again. He always told himself that he just wasn't good enough, that he didn't try hard enough, and that if only he could finally get it right, she would love him completely and forever. Let's call this part The Child. The reason that this part became repressed, and eventually an Ego State, was that this unqualified love for the mother led to disaster. She was so unavailable and so cruel that trying to love her was fundamentally self-destructive. So the love had to be denied, and The Child had to be banished from consciousness.

MOM

Second, there had to be an introjection (a mental representation) of the actual mother. She was so dangerous that it necessitated, within his own mind, a constant reminding of what she liked and what she hated, what she would tolerate and what she would ridicule. In other words, he needed a voice inside his own head that could constantly warn him about the consequences of displeasing her.

Had he not been able to create a mental Part like this, his life would have been much worse. He would have been forever incurring her wrath, doing the wrong thing, simply because he had forgotten the rules and the harsh consequences. He could almost never afford to do "what came naturally" — to obey his instincts — because they included so many things that to her were horrid and filthy and above all, male.

So the voice had to be always at the ready, always on guard, for his own protection. When he got close to misbehaving, it had to chastise, to threaten, so that he could avoid the awful impact of her censure, which was so much worse. Call this part Mom. (It may seem strange that a male can have Parts that are female. However, this is typically the case. And conversely, women usually have a male Part or two.)

Mom exercised her control through guilt. If any of the Parts, or Bob himself, started to get out of hand, she would cause them to feel the same gut-wrenching reaction that the mother did and quickly bring them to their knees. Throughout Bob's psyche, there was a readiness to accept guilt because he had been brainwashed to believe in his essential badness. Convinced as he was that he was lower than a worm, he was a sucker for this. Guilt was the perfect whip.

Mom also served another critical role: as a Jailer. She had to keep all the other Parts properly repressed. This she also accomplished through guilt. If they threatened to get out into consciousness, she laid it on them, and back they went scurrying for cover.

There is a crucial paradox inherent in these roles. On the one hand, she is a protector, and yet she inflicts punishment and enforces imprisonment. How then are the repressed Parts going to react to her? As their colleague and helper because she protects? Hardly. What they are much more keenly aware of over a long period of time is her harshness and oppressiveness, which is the predominant behavior that they observe. They soon forget that it is her job, and a necessary one. Before long, she is The Enemy. A tragically unfair perception on their part, but how else could they be expected to feel?

The reason that Mom had to be driven out of consciousness was a little different than for the other Parts. It was not that she preserved memories of traumas. Rather, it was because she could not possibly fulfill her function if she were part of Bob's conscious mind. He would then have to be aware of what she was doing — repressing all the others — and the whole process would be exposed. So she had to operate from underground in the darkness of secrecy. Even though she basically ran his life for him, he never knew that she existed!

SPORT

Third, there was the athletic Part. It sure didn't want to be a priest, and it, in isolation, didn't care that much about pleasing mom. It just loved to play, and to play well. It enjoyed the grace of a great move in basketball, hitting a home run, and the simple pleasure of having all his body parts work together smoothly. This part, in fact, was a lot more able to enjoy itself when it was able to separate from the rest of Bob, so that he could focus just on the doing of the thing, and for a while not worry about what anyone thought of him. We'll call this part Sport.

The reason for its banishment was that it enjoyed itself too much. Bob learned very early on that he dare not have too much fun, at least not in his mother's presence.

Somehow, for her, pleasure equaled sin. And sin was always followed by guilt-whipping. So fun and pleasure became very dangerous, if they were detectable. In time, his childhood laughter turned into a nervous titter, and his insides tightened at the very thought of unbridled joy.

THE MASON

Fourth, there was the Part that became good at mechanical things. It also preferred being separate for the same reasons as Sport. Call this part The Mason. It was repressed due to a series of incidents that will be related on pages 41-44.

THE KNOWER

The fifth part was in some ways the most troublesome because it was the part that knew the truth about what happened to Bob during his young years. This part didn't develop until Bob began to notice that his mom was not really as nice as the women at church thought she was. It noticed that not all moms made fun of their sons, and not all of the boys were hated for being male.

It was also the part that kept track of all the feelings that Bob had, but was never allowed to act on. It knew all about his Dark Side: jealousy, hatred, anger, lust, and all the rest that mom would not hear of. Not that this part could permit these things to be expressed, but it noted their existence and was aware of the chasm between what Bob felt and what he pretended to feel. This part didn't trust his mom, didn't even like her. It stored away lots of painful memories about her that could not be revealed to any other part.

So in some sense, this part saw the negative side of the family with much greater clarity and accuracy than any other. We'll call this part The Knower. It had to be repressed because it knew too much.

THERAPY — EARLY SESSION

Now we're going to look in on a session after several months of therapy. We had begun using hypnosis several sessions earlier, and Bob had proved quite adept at it. None of the Parts described above had yet surfaced, but during the week he had a dream involving a baby who seemed to be quite neglected. During hypnosis, I asked if the baby represented a Part of Bob, and if so, would he care to make something known to us. The baby was unable to talk, but Bob had a vivid image of the baby again, just as in the dream. The infant looked so neglected and pitiful that it caused Bob to weep and to want to care for it.

After some minutes of this, an unfamiliar sound came out of Bob's mouth, and he began to moan softly. The crying stopped, and a barely audible voice speaking very slowly said, "Don't worry. He's okay. He's feeling a little rough today,but I'll see to it that he gets everything he needs."

I asked, "Who am I talking to?"

She said, "You can call me 'Mom.'"

I asked what her role was in Bob's life, and she said, "I am mostly the baby's caretaker, but I do other things, too. Can't tell you much about that right now."

She asked me who I was and I told her. I also told her a little about what we were trying to do in the therapy and asked for her support. She said she would have to get to know me a lot better before she could promise any such thing. I asked if she knew of any other Parts besides her and the baby, and she once again declined further comment. I then asked why the baby appeared so neglected in the dream, and she said, "Oh, that's somebody trying to make out like I don't do my job well enough. They're always on me, criticizing me, making me look bad."

When I asked why anyone would want to do that, she said with a peculiar, wry smile on her lips, "How would I know? You'll have to ask *them* about that!" She seemed to be implying that she could prevent that from happening — that she was powerful enough to stop them from contacting me.

As it turned out, she was right. It was several months before any of the others were able to speak directly during hypnosis. Their presence in dreams was clear, but she was able to forestall any direct communication.

I then proceeded to tell her in greater detail what we were trying to do. "The first thing I want you to know is that you are welcome here. As far as I'm concerned, you are just as important a part of Bob's internal family as anyone else. I can see that some others don't share that opinion, and we need to find out about that eventually. But I'll bet you that a lot of the reason they don't like you is that they don't really understand you, or what you've been through, or why you have to do what you do in Bob's life.

"If you would be willing to come out and talk some more and to gradually tell us your whole story, I can pretty much promise you that they will stop hating you. I know that for you to tell me the whole truth about yourself will put you in jeopardy and make you vulnerable. But what should be happening at the same time is that the others will be doing likewise — telling us *their* stories. So you won't be the only vulnerable one. Once you all know each other a lot better, some of the hostilities and distrust will melt away. Not only that, but you will find that the one you all serve and care for — Bob — will feel better. He'll be less tense, he'll have more energy, and he'll be extremely grateful to every one of you."

After a long pause, she said, "Well, I'll think about it. But don't be looking for any miracles."

I assured her that I would not and that I looked forward to being able to talk further with her. She then said that she wanted to go rest, and I said okay, that I would count up to five, and Bob would be back in control.

Upon his "return," Bob was visibly unsettled. He had been entirely conscious during the proceedings and was more than a little shocked to hear "this voice" coming out of his mouth. We had talked about this possibility at length earlier, but when it actually happened it was of course quite a jolt to his sensibilities. He reported that the strongest feelings he had were two: First, there was an intense affection for the baby, and second, a profound dislike for the Mom part.

I then asked if he wanted to go ahead with what I had suggested, and he said yes — that even though he was currently distraught, it felt right to him.

A Part like Mom (or like Josie, above) is usually the one who has to be dealt with first because she controls access to everyone else. A particular incident taught me something about this the hard way. When I first met her, I had assured her that I understood and sympathized with her need to keep everyone else under wraps. I also said that I hoped in time to be able to talk with them at length, as that was necessary for the therapy to be beneficial.

So we struck a deal. She would allow the States to make themselves known to me a little at a time, on one condition: that everyone recognize that she had to have ultimate control over when and how much they revealed to me. Yes, we could talk; but only as long and as much as Bob could stand to hear. And she seemed to be in the best position to determine those limitations. It also had to be up to her to decide who would talk when. That seemed reasonable to me, and so I gave her my promise and made the request of the other States that they do likewise.

The very next session I made a major blunder. I was in the habit of saying, "Okay, whoever is in the best position to show us what needs to come next, go ahead." And on this occasion, I said much the same thing. All I knew was that it got very quiet for about ten minutes. But of course this was not at all unusual at the beginning.

The next thing I knew, a voice that sounded like Mom was saying, "Shut up and get back in there! You too! Get back! Get back!"

Then it was very quiet again. Finally it dawned on me what I had done. I had reneged on my promise. Unintentionally so, but I had done it. When I said, "Whoever . . . go ahead," it opened Pandora's Box, and all the Parts came rushing out like kids at recess! This put Mom in a terrible position, and she had to quell a major uprising that was my fault. I apologized immediately, explaining that I had not meant to do it, that it was just a habit. She was sullen for a while, but she soon seemed to realize that it really was accidental. The crisis was over, but it taught me a lesson I wouldn't soon forget.

Over the course of the next year, each of the five Parts described above was allowed to reveal itself, and we had many opportunities to talk with them. It was as though they had been locked away in some secret compartment of the brain for a very long time, and they relished the opportunity to finally get out and interact with someone and to tell their stories.

As you might imagine, they told of a great deal of internal distrust, fear, and mutual hatred. The Child, for example, wanted no part of what The Knower had to say because it found unbearable the idea that mother was anything but perfect. The Knower, for its part, found the Child to be stupid, obsequious, and self-destructive. Mom, in order to perform her function effectively, relied on some degree of allegiance to the real-life mother, and so she too hated The Knower. She thought it vengeful, cynical, and needlessly accusatory. The Knower, of course, thought just as poorly of Mom as he did the biological mother. So there was pitched battle between these two also. General mayhem abounded.

Most of this year of therapy was spent getting to know all these Parts. This is not a quick process. Each Part has its own cache of painful memories, and these can only come into consciousness a little at a time. By the end of the year however, we felt that all the Parts had been contacted, and that each was slowly gaining in strength as they were enabled to participate increasingly in Bob's conscious life. Previously, during the time they were locked away, they could only come out during dreaming or when Bob was overly stressed, so that his defenses were partially neutralized. Gradually, once they showed themselves, he was much more tolerant of their participating in his daily life — particularly if he had some idea of what to expect of them.

This process of coming out often began in the therapy setting. Once I could tell that a given Part was growing and getting stronger, I would suggest that it might want to open its eyes and take a look around. They would do this slowly, with trepidation. When the eyes would first open, they would always squint and say that the light was quite painful. The lighting was actually dim, but to their unaccustomed eyes it hurt. But they were nearly always grateful for the opportunity to see directly through Bob's eyes.

Even with all the Parts out in the open, there was still a good deal of conflict. Each one was still sure that it alone had the best solution to all of Bob's problems, the most accurate perception of the world, and the sole means to helping him lead a happy, satisfying life. This is a very important point: Each and every one of the Parts is truly looking out for what it considers to be Bob's best interest. Every one of them cares deeply for him. They are devoted to him and are trying their best to help him.

The problem comes about because they see such totally different parts of the elephant, and from such conflicting points of view, that they have to fight each other bitterly. It seems so clear to each that the others are going to damage Bob if left to their own devices. So each feels the necessity to assume the leadership role — not because of a selfish lust for power — but because they truly believe they can serve him best. In a sense, it is only because of their loyalty that this kind of therapy can work. Each Part will only loosen its grip, and allow the others to play some active role, if they can be convinced that the person will actually be helped by it and not before.

THERAPY — MIDDLE SESSION

We now look in on a session after about a year and a half of work. At the beginning of each session, before hypnosis begins, I try to get some idea of what is happening in his life, both in terms of actual events and in terms of what he is dreaming about. In this case (again fictitious, but a composite of real events), Bob had told me about a dream in which a wicked witch is under attack. Some others are trying to kill her and to rob her of her mystical powers.

Bob is in a reclined position, and I have asked him to take a minute just to relax. That is by now all that is required for hypnotic "induction." I then say, "Okay. It sounds like Mom is being attacked by some of the others. How can we best proceed?"

There is silence for several minutes, and then a soft voice emerges, speaking in halting, unsteady fashion, which I recognize as Mom. (During the previous months, her voice had become much more confident, even haughty. But at this point, the others were beginning to challenge her tyrannical power, as we'll see.)

Mom: "They hate me. They're not going to stop until they have eliminated me. Most of the time now I leave them alone. I don't know why they can't do the same for me."

Me: "How are they attacking you?"

Mom: "They've taken control of the Child away from me. They've filled his head with garbage about how terrible I am and how he can have so much more fun doing things with them. You know, I suppose that YOU had a lot to do with this. By listening to the others, you let them out of hiding, and so they got stronger. And the stronger they got, the more power they had to fight against me. So first they weakened my grip on the Child, and now he's gone forever. I hope you're satisfied! We'll all probably fry in Hell thanks to you!"

Me: "What's the Child doing when he's with them?"

Mom: "He spends most of his time with the Mason, thinking he's having a great time learning about how to fix things. But the Knower is around him a lot, too, giving his sick version of what his poor mother was like. And of course, he's so young and impressionable that he believes a lot of it."

Me: "I know I've told you this before, but I'm going to say it again. They can't kill you. It just isn't possible. I don't know why, but I have never seen it happen, and I don't expect to this time either. I still say that, as the others get to know you better, they'll see what a valuable function you have performed for Bob.

"You had a really ugly job to do, one that got you into a lot of trouble with the others, but somebody HAD to do it. It's just like in a society: Somebody has to collect the garbage, and somebody has to guard the jails. There's nothing very pretty about either, but society couldn't exist without people to do those things. You're no different. You're not a bad Part. You just got stuck with a dirty job and all the stigma and isolation that goes with it. One day the others will have some compassion for that and will realize that they need to support you, at least emotionally.

"In fact, I want to ask them about that now: Is there anybody who is in a position to help Mom right now? Can you begin to see that she is NOT the enemy, but that she is a legitimate part of this family just like the rest of you?"

Mom: (After a long pause.) "The Knower just looked at me. That's not much, but it's the first time he has ever even acknowledged my existence in a direct way. And to tell you the truth, it wasn't a mean look like I expected. It was more like he was studying me, trying to grasp something about me. It scared me at first, but it feels okay now."

Me: "That's what we were hoping for."

Mom: "Well, I'm real tired. That was really quite a scare. I think I want to stop for now."

Me: "Okay. But before we stop, is there anybody else who wants to say anything?"

Knower: (Silence for about half a minute, then there is a

slightly deeper voice, a different speech cadence, and pronunciation that is more clipped): "Maybe she's not such a bitch after all. I guess before, when I was much weaker, I was afraid of her. That's a lot of why I wouldn't look at her. But she still seems dangerous to me. I mean, why does she have to keep making the Child feel guilty all the time, like he's a rotten kid?"

Me: "Now wait a minute. Isn't it true that she does that less now?"

Knower: "Yeah, I suppose so. It's just that after so many decades of the same thing, it's hard to trust her."

Me: "I know. But the fact is that the internal balance of power has actually shifted somewhat and you other guys are much more able to influence the Child in other ways now. True?"

Knower: "Yeah, I suppose. Well, we'll try to give her the benefit of the doubt. I guess she has been all alone a long time. Kind of sad in a way, even for a witch."

Me: "There may come a time when she will be able to return the favor. I hope so. Anything else you wanted to say?"

Knower: "No. I think we've got plenty to work on for now."

Me: "Okay. I'm going to count up to five, and Bob will be fully grown and back in this room."

When Bob sits up, he is awake and has heard everything that went on. If there was any kind of pain to be felt, he was also aware of that, in a direct way. So we take a little time to process what happened before he leaves. For him, and for nearly all clients who do hypnosis (and to some extent for me also), there is afterward a sense of having left one time zone and entered another. One feels a bit of confusion and disorientation. There is also frequently a sense of "Did that really happen? What the devil was it, and what does it mean?" Walking from the darkened office out into the sunlight is often a bit of a shock and leaves both of us wondering which world is more real.

During the next year, the work continued in much the same way. At one point, Bob began having splitting head-aches whenever he tried to do woodworking or any of the maintenance activities the Mason was so good at. In trance, the Mason told the following story:

"When Bob was little, his mom left him alone a lot, which was fine with me. I never cared for her anyway. And it gave us time to learn all sorts of things. When Bob was about ten, we learned how to fix bicycles. His dad had the right tools; and since he was never home, we could use them anytime we wanted. You know me — I got good at it.

"Well, there were these twin girls about Bob's age in the neighborhood who got secondhand bikes for Christmas. The family was poor, and the bikes were cheap and were always breaking down. So of course Bob (and I) became their knight in shining armor. They'd break 'em ahd we'd fix 'em. What fun! They were cute too, and Bob had a crush on one of them.

"Then one day the twin he liked best showed up alone at his house after school. Her bike seemed to be okay, so I couldn't figure out what she wanted. Pretty soon she started — you know — kissing him and stuff like that. I can tell you Bob was liking it all right!

"But then all of a sudden, his mother appears out of nowhere. She starts screaming at the girl to get out of her house and never, ever come back, and that she is going to call her mother and tell her what a little tramp she's rais-ing. The girl runs.

"Then she starts on Bob. She demands to know every-thing about what has been going on to lead up to this. She seems to want to hear every single, gory detail, but then she acts like she is so disgusted she's going to puke. Anyway, he tells all — about how he fixed their bikes, how he started liking the girl, everything. She tells him that he is going to burn in Hell, and what did she do to deserve such a horrid son, and that he had better never breathe a word of this to anyone, not even at confession. The priests would never let any member of the family back in the church if they knew about all this sickening sexual perversion.

"Bob looked like he had been whipped half to death and stayed like that for a long time. The next day, Bob had a very bad headache, the first time he ever had one that bad. After school, he wandered down into the basement where his dad kept the tools, and there was this new cabinet. All the tools were in it, and it had a padlock on it. There was a note in his mother's handwriting. It said: "Tools are not for nasty boys to play with." All of a sudden, the headache intensified, and Bob could hardly see. It stayed that way for a couple days.

"Bob didn't seem interested in girls for quite a while after that. But the worst thing for me was that every time he would try to pick up a tool, even in wood shop at school, he would get this terrible pain in his head. The teacher finally arranged for him to have a study period while the other guys learned woodworking. I was heartsick. After that, he didn't touch a tool for almost ten years. It wasn't until his was in the Army and was forced to do some maintenance that he let me out at all. Even then, the headaches still came. Not as bad as before, but they hurt a lot. Just a minute . . ." (By this time, the Mason is crying hard and holding his head where the pain is. In between sobs, the story continues.)

"That's why he's been having the headaches recently when he's working. I felt like he was finally strong enough to handle hearing the story and feeling the pain. So there it is." (After a few minutes, the sobbing ceases, and he becomes very still.)

"That reminds me: you used to ask me why I hated the part you call Mom. Well, during that ten years, I would sometimes get up the nerve to push Bob toward a tool, knowing how much we always loved doing that stuff. Every time he would get within reach, Mom would blast him with that same splitting headache, and he would run away again. For a long time, I couldn't see that she was doing her job. I thought she just plain hated us, that she liked to inflict pain and to keep us away from things we loved doing. I can see now that if she had not done it, and if we had gotten caught again by his real mom, it would have been curtains. So she really was trying to protect us, in a backhanded kind of way. Anyway, I'm glad it's finally out. I feel better, and I think pretty soon Bob will, too."

He did. Within a couple of weeks, he bought a few basic tools and was talking about how much money he could save doing his own work on the house.

I include this story partly to show how it is that learning about each other's history makes the Parts more tolerant of one another. And partly as an example of how physical pain is often a clue to a memory. I have seen many patients develop unaccountable pains and bruises, only to subsequently learn that these parts of the body were beaten, or were wounded during sexual abuse, or some such. Once the memories were out in the open, and the pain was experienced, the bruises would disappear within a day or so. If you find that bizarre, I don't blame you. Not so many years ago, I would have scoffed at such a story. I've now seen it so often I take it for granted.

SEXUAL TRAUMA

I want to include one other intermediate session in order to describe what actually happens when someone is in the process of reliving a sexual trauma.

Bob is in trance. Mom has been talking about how she has felt terrible all week. She is very nervous and obviously frightened. There is silence for a few minutes. Then she starts saying how lucky Bob was to go to a church where the priests were very strict and how much he needed that kind of control. Bob's legs begin to shake. Just a little at first, but then violently, almost as though he is having a seizure.

Mom: "What's going on here? Can't you make him stop?" (Then screams:) "Get away from me! Leave me alone! No! No!" The shaking continues unabated for nearly five minutes. She is now sobbing, intermixed with the screams of "No, no, no!" Finally the sobbing and the screams subside, and the body is very still. Eventually a very weak voice says, "Get me out of here."

[I have an agreement with everyone who does hypnosis that when they say anything like that, I will immediately count up to five and get them out, no questions asked. There are also many times when my counting is not necessary, when they themselves terminate the trance quite abruptly.]

After another five minutes of rest, I asked Bob if it was anything he wanted to tell me about. He said he simply could not, but maybe later. He was so exhausted that he was unable to drive, so I called his wife and she came to get him.

During the next session, he was able to tell me part of what had happened:

Bob: "I was at school. It was before Easter, and we were getting ready to do a play. Father (one of the priests at the school) said he wanted me to try out for the Jesus part and that I would need to wear a loincloth to make it real. He told me to take off my pants and try on the cloth to see if it would fit. I felt real strange, but I did as I was told. I always did as I was told.

"When I was trying on the loincloth, he came over to me and started 'adjusting' it. In the process, he put his hand on my penis. He said he had to see if it was big enough to where I could play the role of a man. I thought I was going to faint. I remember I got real dizzy, and my legs started to collapse. But I couldn't let that happen. I made my legs real rigid so I wouldn't fall. I kept them that way the whole time.

"I couldn't believe this was happening to me. I couldn't believe that Father would ever do anything like this. But there he was, doing it. Not only that, but I remembered him having this look on his face that I had never seen before. He was blushing, and I know his hands were trembling. I could just barely see his face because he stopped looking up at me and was concentrating on the 'adjustments.'"

Me: "Did he threaten you if you told?"

Bob: "Oh God, yes. First he told me that this was nothing unusual, that all try-outs were held in this way. But toward the end, his expression changed, and he said, 'I forgive you for your part in this, but if you ever tell anyone, I will personally see to it that you go straight to Hell.'

"I was just a young kid, and I most certainly believed he could do that. I also had a very vivid picture of what Hell was like, including burning flesh and gnashing teeth. So he had me. It's like he knew just how to get me. It was perfect. But when he said, 'I forgive *you* . . .' what the devil did he mean by that?"

Me: "It was another perfect way to get you. He made you feel like you were equally to blame for what had happened. Children think that if they were there at the scene of the crime and didn't stop what had happened from happening, then they must be partly to blame. They can't seem to tolerate the idea of being completely helpless. Like you, they also can't conceive that this adult is actually doing such a thing to them because everybody thinks the adult is just fine. So if the adult is fine, then the culprit has to be the child. Cunning. And very effective. You kept your mouth shut for about twenty years. How are you now?"

Bob: "Still shaky. I've been shaking on and off all week. Over and over, I've said to myself, 'That bastard DID that to me.' And then a minute later, I'd be thinking, Oh, sure. Like that really happened. Don't be ridiculous! You know what an overactive imagination you have. You're in therapy, and you're always looking for someone you can blame your problems on."

Me: "Did the voice sound familiar?"

Bob: "Oh yeah. I knew right away it was Mom. Remember last week when she started screaming, 'Get away, leave me alone' and all that? Well, she wasn't screaming at you. She was screaming at The Knower. He was starting to bring this stuff up to where I could see and feel it, and she couldn't bear the thought. She was still convinced I really would burn in Hell. I can sure understand now why she was fearful for me — there were times last week when I thought I was dying, that I had gotten in over my head and there was no way out. I've never been so scared in all my life."

As it turned out, we were still not finished with the incident. In their turn, a whole range of emotions and physical reactions made their way to the surface. First, there was the disbelief that this could happen at all. Then there was a sense of rage: against the priest, against the church, against God — everybody connected with authority in any way. The authority that was supposed to protect him but didn't. There was also the terrible frustration of having to lock away this poisonous secret for so many years, mixed with a profound disappointment in his family because they had not somehow known or sensed what had happened to him.

All this came out gradually over several weeks. Bob felt miserable and very ashamed during most of it. Finally, however, it dawned on him that he was *not* a willing participant, and that it was in no way his fault. This fact more than any other seemed to lift the spell, and he was able to place the blame squarely where it belonged — on the perpetrator.

Not long afterward, he was able to make sense out of the fact that he had always carried in his heart a profound feeling of distress and a strange fear of being found out. *What* was going to be found out had never been specified, but the feeling was so strong that it didn't need to be corroborated by any facts. For the first time since childhood, he began to consider the possibility that maybe he wasn't any worse than other people. Not that he was anything great, but maybe he wasn't slime. It was a start.

Bob had been an ideal target for this priest.* He was someone who did as he was told. He was taught to respect authority unquestioningly. He had a morbid fear of Hell. Lastly, and very importantly, he lacked a father. These qualities fit nicely with a pedophile's needs. They make certain children safe victims.

Now let's look in on one of his last sessions. We are now a little more than three years into the therapy:

THERAPY — LAST SESSION

Me: "Seems like we're getting close to your being able to continue this work on your own. How does everybody feel about that?"

Child: "It feels odd to hear you refer to us as 'everybody.' Sure, we're still divided in some ways, but in other ways we're just one person. Sport will never be as good a craftsman as the Mason, and Mom and the Knower will probably never see exactly eye to eye on how Bob's mother treated him, but still we're a lot more unified. I don't have to be afraid that Mom is going to try to control my every movement. She lets me do mostly what I want, within reason. But she's always there to warn me if I get dangerously frisky. And to tell you the truth, I've come to see that I need that. It's just not in my nature to be cautious, and it's comforting to know that somebody is looking over my shoulder, watching out for me."

Mason: (After a few moments of silence, some shifting.) "Yeah, I'm really grateful to her for stopping the headaches. But I've come to see that I sort of rely on her, too. I get so involved in what I'm doing that

* I'm not trying to pick on priests or on the Catholic Church. It could just as well have been an Evangelist or a Mormon, or a nurse, a policeman, or a housepainter. Pedophilia cuts across all social boundaries.

"BOB" ❖ 49

I lose track of the ways these tools can actually hurt me. And she's good about keeping track. We all need her, I think. One of the things she can do now is let us help each other. Before, I guess she had to keep us separated — it was easier for her to maintain control over individuals than over a group. But now, we often work together. I like it a lot better."

Mom: (Another period of silence.) "I think the greatest surprise of all for me was to discover that I had feelings. For over forty years, I had zero opportunity to pay any attention to what I might feel. I had to be continually keeping the others under my thumb and stayed so exhausted from it I never had the energy for anything else. I had actually begun thinking of myself as the same cold hard bitch the others saw.

"Then when they began maturing, and it became safe for me to rest once in a while, that's when the feelings showed up. Maybe they were there all along, but I sure didn't know about them. Funny how staying real busy keeps you from feeling anything."

Sport: (Again, after a silence.) "I can still remember the first time I ever saw you cry. It was when you realized that you might have actually hurt The Child by keeping him so locked up and frozen. When he first came out and you actually looked at him, you could see how sickly and undeveloped he was, and it hurt you to think you did it to him. That was the beginning of my changing my feelings toward you. I had always believed you were pure nasty and mean. Seeing you cry made me think you must have had some reason for what you did, because you sure didn't enjoy The Child's being in so much pain."

The Child: (Another pause.) "Well, I'm feeling much better, thanks. I don't hold it against her anymore either.

I just feel very lucky to have finally gotten out. I can tell that I'm still a little weak and that some of you guys have to take over for me when we get into complicated situations.

"But I've also learned that I have something to contribute that is of value. I can get positively tickled about something, just like a little kid. It's really fun! I'm not weighed down by all the worries about work and stuff like you guys, so I can just enjoy whatever it is without those distractions. I know how much you enjoy seeing me able to do that, and I think you get something out of it, too. But you're always there in case I get carried away, which I often seem to do!

"Another thing I can do better than any of you is relate to little kids since I'm basically one myself. I understand them lots better than the rest of you, and that is going to be real nice for any children that Bob might want to have later."

Me: "Sound like your life has improved in a number of ways. I'm delighted for you."

Knower: "Yeah, most of the time. But we've all learned that life kicks you in the teeth periodically, and we're not kidding ourselves about that anymore. There is always going to be plenty of pain to contend with — that's just how it is. But we've found that being willing to suffer the pain allows us to feel really good sometimes also. And that's what makes it worthwhile.

"There are also times when we can still get into serious conflict with each other. I think the difference now is that we know that there really is more than one way to see things, and we're willing to at least hear each other out. Then, collectively, we try to come to some compromise about what's best. Each of us used to try to be a dictator. Now it's more like a democracy. I think it works a lot better. We all thank you for your help."

POSTSCRIPT:

I need to add some immediate qualifiers to this account. First, therapy is not always this successful or this fast. It seems to depend on a host of factors. Did the person have someone in his life who really loved him? If so, it seems to give them a strength and a sense of security that not everyone has. Does he have the emotional and financial resources to allow him to obtain a reasonable amount of what he wants and needs? If so, it makes life easier. Did the person suffer so much trauma that it is intolerable for him to bring it back to awareness? I think many people, sadly, cannot endure this sort of therapy. The cure can prove to be worse than the illness in such cases. Do the person and therapist have a fair amount in common — enough so that the person feels truly understood most of the time? If not, therapy is not likely to succeed.

Therapy with ESD patients is very similar to Family Therapy. In working with families, one usually finds that much of the problem has to do with misunderstanding. A parent fails to understand a child partly because it has been a great while since he was one, and he has had to put so much of that behind him. The child fails to understand the parent because he/she has never been there. Thus much of the work involves getting people to switch places — to put themselves in the other person's shoes, so as to comprehend as much as they can about the other's inner life. This is exactly what occurs in work with Ego States. Once they can empathize with each other, the conflicts begin to dissolve.

THERAPY OUTCOME

While good things can come about as a result of this work, I don't want to pretend that it is the cure for all of life's problems. Decreasing the amount of internal conflict allows the possibility of greater peace of mind, but it does not guarantee happiness. Purging pain from the unconscious diminishes bodily tension and anxiety, but it by itself does not ensure satisfaction with one's life. Regaining years of lost memories is very helpful in making sense of who we are, but it is still up to us to mold that into something we can like and respect. And even if we are fortunate enough to accomplish that, we will only feel it some portion of the time. Neither this therapy nor any other can deliver us permanently from self-doubt, sadness, and occasionally even abject misery. But what we can reasonably hope for is an improvement in the balance. That seems to me what makes it worthwhile.

People do not enter into this kind of therapy on a whim or because of minor irritations in their lives like boredom or job dissatisfaction. They do not awaken one day and say, "Gee, it's about time I attended to those awful things I know I have forgotten about." Rather, they come when they have to. It is usually their bodies that force them. Sometimes it can be nightmares which remind them of something they know they must come to terms with or a divorce that tears away from them many of their usual defenses. But usually it is the body that takes over, sending powerful signals which cannot be ignored. These include such things as panic attacks, unbearable headaches, and a general conviction that they are having a nervous breakdown. It is only when things get this bad that we are willing to go through what we sense will be a long and painful healing process. In a way, it's a shame that it has to get to this point. But as long as our repressive forces are working satisfactorily, we much prefer to just forget the past, or at least the most hurtful portions of it.

Although I think that this kind of therapy is well suited to this disorder, it still requires a great expenditure of time and money. I wish it were faster, but the truth is that it takes a number of years in most cases. And even then the work is not likely to be entirely finished. The therapy itself is partly a teaching process in which one learns how to help oneself. Possibly the most important single thing that is learned is to listen to one's body, to one's feelings.

After a while, these can serve much the same guiding function that the therapist fulfilled earlier. Initially, most people have so little faith in what they feel that the therapist has to almost force them to pay attention to it and to inquire into what the body is trying to say. Little by little, they begin to see that it really is trustworthy. In a most fundamental way, this means that they are not crazy. Their feelings really are connected directly to reality. They reflect it, and they tell us important things about it. It often requires some diligence to find out what the body's message is. But when this is done successfully a number of times, they begin to have real confidence in the process.

I hope that by now the concept of Ego State Disorder has begun to make some sense. If so, perhaps we can proceed to flesh it out more fully and to examine some related issues.

It should be noted that the term "disorder" is in some ways misleading in describing this condition. It suggests that Ego States are a form of psychiatric problem, that they constitute the disorder. But it is important to be aware that in some sense they are really the solution to a problem — the problem being the abuse itself, and the dissociating into Ego States being the means by which the person is enabled to survive.

CHAPTER IV

HYPNOTIC TRANCE AND ALTERED STATES OF MIND

In order to understand how hypnosis is used in the treatment of Ego State Disorder, we first need to understand something about the nature of trance in general. Trance is not some singular, clearly identifiable state of mind. There is instead a great variety of kinds of trance. True, they do tend to have certain things in common, but they also have a great many differences.

Many times hypnosis done in clinical offices is simply relaxation training or encouraging the client to concentrate on images that come to mind. For many clients, that is probably as close as they can come to being hypnotized. Debate has raged for more than a hundred years over issues such as:

"Is everyone hypnotizable?"

"What happens when you are hypnotized?"

"Is the experience the same for everyone?"

The first and last of these questions can probably be answered with some degree of certainty.

No, everyone is not hypnotizable. Ernest Hilgard (1986) and many others have come to this conclusion after decades of careful scientific inquiry. Estimates range from 20 percent to over 50 percent, depending on the degree of hypnotizability used as the criterion. There is within the hypnotizable group a much smaller subgroup of persons who are *highly* hypnotizable. These persons are readily able to be hypnotically regressed, for example, and to recover events from the distant past with striking accuracy (later verified independently). He describes these as "hypnotic virtuosos." They constitute somewhere between one percent and five percent of the population.

No, the experience of hypnosis is not the same for everyone. Some people describe the sense of becoming increasingly detached from their bodies; others say precisely the opposite. Some describe it as "going down" into some other state, while others say they feel that they are floating or are nowhere in particular. Trance can be induced by relaxation, but in many hypnotizable persons, it can be induced just as well by increased activation! So there is no such thing as a "paradigmatic trance experience."

But neither is it accurate to say that we can *only* describe it as an "altered state." It is more consistent than that. Hilgard (pp. 163-164) lists four features that are fairly reliable:

1. Increased suggestibility. For many years, this was considered to be the cornerstone of trance experience. However, he notes that ". . . these changes . . . alone provide a very limited characterization of the total alterations . . . "

2. Enhanced imagery and imagination, including the availability of visual memories from the past. He sees this as being the crux of the trance experience. He also notes that this particular capacity for *imaginative involvement* is the one factor which best predicts whether a given person will be hypnotizable or not. "The person who becomes temporarily involved sets ordinary reality aside as he becomes totally absorbed in the imaginative experience." (p. 160)

3. Subsidence of the planning function. "The hypnotized subject loses initiative and lacks the desire to make

and carry out plans of his own." This is of course a temporary state and ceases as soon as the person becomes alert
again.

4. Reduction in reality testing. Time sometimes stands
still, sometimes races forward or backward at breakneck
speed. Sometimes the person feels his current age and is
sometimes thoroughly convinced that he is three or four.
People seem much more intent on what they *feel* and have
less concern for how or whether that fits in with current
reality. Orne (1959) has coined the phrase "trance logic" to
describe this tendency to suspend ordinary logic and to
replace it with one that does indeed have a certain consis-
tency, but obeys quite a different set of rules.

It bears repeating that trance is always a matter of
degree. A client may go "in" and "out" of various hypnotic
depths during any given session. Interestingly enough, most
clients can tell you, in some numerical way, approximately
where they are in terms of depth. And the telling does
nothing to disturb wherever they are. They may start out
by muttering, "I just can't seem to do this today," only to
find themselves moments later thrust quite involuntarily
into a horrible childhood memory, describing everything in
startling detail from the wallpaper pattern to the smell of
grandpa's cologne. They may spend five minutes in this
time period, only to abruptly yank themselves into full
consciousness in the present. Those five minutes may have
been all that they could stand at that time.

Had they, or I, tried to force them to stay longer, the
hypnotic process would have spontaneously aborted. This is
accomplished either by vomiting or by their brains emitting
enough endorphines to neutralize the experience by pro-
ducing a mild state of shock. (This is explained in Chapter
VI.) The latter is probably what happened at the time of the
original trauma.

THE HIDDEN OBSERVER

Hilgard has been studying hypnotic phenomena in the laboratory for over half a century. But it was one of his students who made one of the most important discoveries, dubbed "The Hidden Observer." In a classroom demonstration, Hilgard had induced hypnotic deafness in a subject. He was told that at the count of three he would become completely deaf to all sounds and that his hearing would be restored when the instructor's hand was placed on his right shoulder. Hilgard counted to three. Loud sounds were then made close to the subject's head by banging wooden blocks together, and there was no sign of any reaction. He had also shown no response to the loud crack of a starter's pistol. Nor did he respond to students' questions.

Although there was no doubt about the temporary state of deafness, an inquisitive student asked if perhaps "some part" of the subject might be aware of what was going on. Hilgard agreed to pursue the possibility and said to the subject:

> "As you know, there are parts of our nervous system that carry on activities that occur out of awareness, of which control of the circulation of the blood, or the digestive process, are most familiar. However, there may be intellectual processes also of which we are unaware, such as those that find expression in night dreams. Although you are hypnotically deaf, perhaps there is some part of you that is hearing my voice and processing the information. If there is, I should like the index finger of your right hand to rise as a sign that this is the case."

To the surprise of the instructor, as well as the class, the finger rose! The subject immediately said:

> "Please restore my hearing so you can tell

me what you did. I felt my finger rise in a way that was not a spontaneous twitch, so you must have done something to make it rise, and I want to know what you did."

Hilgard assured him that he would do so, but that first he wanted to ask another question.

"Does the part to whom I am now talking know more about what went on?"
"Yes."
"Tell me what went on."
"After you counted to make me deaf, you made noises with some blocks behind my head. Members of the class asked me questions to which I did not respond. Then one of them asked if I might not really be hearing, and you told me to raise my finger if I did. This part of me responded by raising my finger, so it's all clear now." (Hilgard, pp. 186-187)

This "part" of the subject which retained its auditory acuity was labeled a "Hidden Observer." This same phenomenon has since been demonstrated repeatedly under the most rigorous experimental controls. One of the most common techniques involves "hypnotic anesthesia." The hypnotized subject places one arm in a bucket of ice water. The water is cold enough so that a nonhypnotized person could not stand it for more than ten or fifteen seconds.

In trance, however, the person seems content to leave it there for many minutes with no sign of discomfort. A pencil is then put in the other hand, and the person is asked to indicate the degree of pain on a scale of one to ten. The numbers depict exactly what would normally be expected — at first the pain is described as minimal, but quickly becomes extreme! If this "other part" of the person is accessed verbally, it will angrily demand that the person be allowed to remove the arm from the bucket because it is damned painful!

Hilgard adds a most interesting postscript to his account of the original discovery:

> It should be noted that the "hidden observer" is a metaphor for something occurring at an intellectual level but not available to the consciousness of the hypnotized person. It does not mean that there is a secondary personality with a life of its own — a kind of homunculus lurking in the shadows of the conscious person. [It] is merely a convenient label for the information source tapped through experiments with automatic writing and automatic talking. (Hilgard, p. 188)

He may be right. There may well be cases where there is a secondary level of awareness that does not qualify as a full-blown secondary *personality*. But for him to imply that this is always the case seems heavy-handed to me. This may be yet another example of the kind of perceptual difference that derives from experimental, as opposed to clinical, background and experience. Curiously enough, later in the same book, he relents this position. In describing the Watkins' (1979-1980) work with Ego States, he says:

> They described an ego state as an enduring fraction of the total personality, like a "covert" or incipient multiple personality. The Watkins' methods yielded hidden observers in all of their subjects and patients. . . . It is understandable that the patients should have assigned the hidden observer to one or more of these acknowledged states. *Perhaps less expected was that within the same person some ego states reported while other ego states denied that they had knowledge of the concealed pain* (or hearing in the study with students). There are clearly some analogies between the hidden observer phenomenon and the ego-

state interpretation, with both representing dissociations. . . . The interpretation of ego states as
incipient multiple personalities is an intriguing
possibility, suggesting that multiple personalities
may be more prevalent than commonly believed.
(p. 300) [my italics]

His use of the word "incipient" is most interesting. It
suggests that Ego States are not stable entities in and of
themselves, but are always evolving in the direction of
becoming Alters in Multiple Personalities. But why should
this be so? Why should they necessarily deteriorate into a
more serious form of disorder? Why can't Ego States just be
Ego States? I think that the answer lies partly in the fact
that Ego State Disorder is not yet officially a reality; it is
not part of the accepted diagnostic schema. We simply have
not yet begun to think of it that way. But it may well be
time for us to begin doing so.

THE NATURE OF HYPNOTIC INDUCTION

There is also quite a different twist to the same general topic. When a therapist "hypnotizes" someone, we are
inclined to assume that *he* is is doing something to the
client and that it is the "induction" that creates this curious
effect in the client. I want to suggest a different view
(proposed by numerous other people as well): that accomplishing trance induction is due much more to the client
than the therapist. Not that the therapist is irrelevant. He
has considerable importance as a companion and a guide.
But what I would maintain is that the vast majority of
people who are hypnotizable *already* know how to create a
trance state before the induction is ever begun. They have
almost invariably learned to do it when they were children,
as suggested by Hilgard (1987). They are able to suspend
selected portions of reality for the moment in order to be
maximally absorbed in whatever they are attending to or

imagining. In some cases, it seems that they were encouraged and trained by parents who were themselves adept at such enterprises.

In other cases, I feel sure that it is an involuntary, natural response to trauma. Nearly all children have the ability to "make themselves go away" into a fantasy world when they are being sexually or physically abused or are being otherwise severely traumatized. If such experiences recur fairly often (as was true for Sally and Bob), it stands to reason that the child would come to feel very safe in such a fantasy world and would frequently escape into it. (If this model is correct, there should be a very high correlation between being hypnotizable and having experienced extensive childhood trauma. Research and clinical data are needed to establish the truth or falsity of this claim.)

How do children learn their own individual styles of hypnosis? One child might find repeated refuge, during abuse, in returning to a scene in which she is swinging quietly on her swing. Another, under similar circumstances, might choose to concentrate on the smell of her grandmother's kitchen — the one place she feels truly safe. Another (somewhat like Sally) might actually bang her head on the floor to the point where she becomes semi-unconscious or at least dizzy enough to escape the immediacy of the abuse.

Thus, "trance induction" for the first person, as an adult, might best be accomplished by encouraging the familiar visual focusing; for the second person by concentrating on smells; and for the third on sudden and jarring physical movements. So why not simply ASK the client the question: "When you were little, where did you go in your mind when you couldn't stand it anymore? What did you do to escape the situation?" Most clients are able to identify this process quite easily (IF they did it) and can then use it to induce trance for themselves. Sometimes they will not know the answer when first asked, but as they encounter increasingly difficult scenes in therapy, they find that they automatically fall back on essentially the same safety-producing maneuvers as they did in childhood. Once these are identified, they can be systematically used for hypnotic induction.

If then, a person comes *into* the therapy setting either able or unable to be hypnotized, what is it that actually happens in the so-called "induction?" I would argue that it is mostly a matter of the client watching the therapist very closely, judging whether or not that person is in fact knowledgeable in that area, and personally able to tolerate any or all of what might come out during the session. I am convinced that the degree of trance that my own clients are able to descend into has a great deal to do with my own psychological state at that particular time. If I am reasonably settled and able to be truly present with them during their journey, then the depth of trance can be much greater than if they sense that I am tense or irritable or preoccupied with my own personal problems. After all, they would be foolhardy to give me trust carte-blanche, knowing that I am human and thus doomed to have "off-days."

One of the things this means is that the therapist should never ask questions which are more probing than he/she is really ready to hear the answer to. If I ask about something very intimate, but am not terribly available emotionally, I put the patient in a difficult bind. She is expected to answer truthfully, but senses that it can go nowhere. So she has to answer in a way that keeps the emotion separated from the response. This in turn leads to a very awkward interaction, and one that is difficult to disentangle. If it happens very often, it also leads to a considerable amount of distrust.

If the foregoing observations about hypnosis are true, it would partially account for the differing accounts of hypnotizability given by clinicians as opposed to experimenters in the laboratory. The former routinely report substantially higher percentages of hypnotizability than the latter. If trance does truly depend partly on trusting the therapist, this apparent difference is exactly what we would expect. Clients almost always have a much more extensive opportunity to get to know a therapist than an experimenter and much more sense of whether or not he or she is trustworthy. Indeed, I have found that some people who are not at all able to be hypnotized when they first begin therapy become quite able to do it after a month of two, or even longer, once trust has been better established.

POST-TRAUMATIC STRESS DISORDER

Another category of "altered states" is contained in a diagnostic category called Post-Traumatic Stress Disorder (PTSD). This state is highly relevant to our purposes. In the case of the solider who lost his leg, we might well find this disorder. If the experience overall was sufficiently traumatic, he may well have repressed some or all of it. What we would expect to find then would be certain sorts of symptom formations. It is fairly likely that he would have nightmares. There could be paralysis in his other compensating limbs. There could well be panic attacks, wherein his heart would race out of control, he would be unable to breathe, and he would feel that he was dying. We might also find depression, agitation, and sleep and/or appetite disturbance.

Hypnosis is considered by many to be the treatment of choice for PTSD. The procedure is deceptively simple, although by no means painless. The person is gradually encouraged to mentally place himself again in the original circumstances. As he does this, he begins to have exactly the same bodily and emotional reactions as occurred then. This is a grueling procedure, evoking as it does the same pains that nearly killed him the first time. A little at a time, he is able to bring to consciousness portions of the experience that have been repressed until finally the entire event is experienced.

I say "experienced" — not "re-experienced." There is a common misconception about therapy that asks "Why re-experience misery? It was bad enough the first time — why dig it up again?" The point is that portions of it never *were* experienced. By the body — yes. By the conscious mind — no. In treatment, they are in fact being experienced for the first time in full awareness. Following this, we would expect the various symptoms to diminish and then gradually disappear.

There is one further image that can help us to understand the nature of trance — something a student of mine dubbed "The Combination Lock." In the incident above, there may well be twenty different events going on simultaneously. Surrounding the trauma itself, there is information coming in from all five senses. So later there are visual, auditory, olfactory, kinesthetic, and possibly even gustatory portions of the memories. There are also a lot of bodily responses that are stored as memories: rapid heartbeat, sweating, ACTH secretion (a hormonal alarm reaction), removal of blood from the stomach and intestines, and finally endorphine secretion. In addition, there are thoughts: it happened on a Tuesday, at twilight, when he was very tired. This extensive array of factors then constitutes what we call "one" experience.

Exactly the same sort of array is present for a child being sexually or physically abused or in any way traumatized. What then happens in trance is that we begin with whatever element(s) of the experience we are presented with, and it leads to others. The person may dream that they are suffocating. We then concentrate on that one feeling. It usually intensifies, becoming closer in magnitude to what it was originally. That typically reaches a temporary peak and then begins to diminish. There is often a brief rest period, followed by gradual emergence of the other factors in their turn.

My impression is that the first things to appear are the least painful and that the last things to appear are the most painful. This results in a curious-looking progression. Rather than begin by systematically restoring the memories from the five sensory modalities, and then proceeding to the hormonal responses, the process seems to jump around randomly. We may start with an awareness of suffocation, leap to a memory of reading a letter from home two days before, and then to a feeling of his heart jumping up into his throat. There may be a logic to this in the sense of proceeding from least to greatest pain, but it is not the sort of progression that we are accustomed to. It can be quite confusing to clients until they follow it through to conclusion a few times.

When I was describing this to an undergraduate class, one of the students said it sounded like trying to find the combination to a lock. Precisely so. The tumbler clicks when the person's heart is accelerated to the same point as it did originally. It clicks again when the feeling of suffocation gets to the correct level of intensity, and so on. And when all, or enough, of the tumblers fall into place, the lock opens, and the experience is restored. In actual practice, it is never quite this neat. But the image is nonetheless quite appropriate.

OTHER ALTERED STATES
IN THERAPY

At one end of the trance continuum are those rare individuals Hilgard described as "hypnotic virtousi." At the other end is a much larger group of people whose trance states are much less "altered" from normal waking states, but which are nonetheless useful in treatment. The approaches are rather different according to the degree of trance. Most persons who go into a typical hypnotic trance become perfectly still, and their breathing slows way down. It is then often possible to speak directly to one or more of the Ego States and to get a direct, verbal response.

At the end of doing this, it usually seems that the person is still in quite a different state of mind (temporally, spatially, and perceptually). For that reason, I always go through a brief ritual of counting from zero up to five to encourage the person back into their fully adult state. (Twice I neglected to do that. One of the people tripped over the door sill going outside. The other sideswiped a tree when leaving the parking area. I've never been certain whether or not those were just coincidences. But now I always count up to five.)

Things are different in milder trances. People do not become motionless, nor does their breathing rate slow down so drastically. It is rarely possible to speak directly to Ego States. (Actually, I do sometimes address them directly. They do not respond back to me verbally, but the ensuing images and bodily sensations often seem clearly responsive to my comments or questions.) Also, there is usually no need to count up to five afterward. However, if the person has been vividly involved in some earlier event in their lives, I may well do it. It is just to establish a clear demarcation between that regressive process and what needs to happen now in terms of going back out into the real world, driving a car, etc.

Even those mildly altered states are very useful, however. Nearly all of those people have proven to be adept at tuning in to messages that are delivered either through bodily sensations, images, or repetitive thoughts. Essentially the same sorts of clues are made conscious as those described in the Combination Lock image. Upon focusing his attention inward, the person may presently observe that one hand feels unusually cold, or that he keeps seeing a certain area where he used to play as a child, or that a particular name reverberates in his head.

The person is then asked to continue concentrating on whatever that is until it changes to something else. We follow this trail of clues, and it typically leads to very bad experiences that were locked out of awareness. So the outcome is much the same. It's just a different way of getting there.

DISSOCIATION: Death and Rebirth of a Concept

Dissociation, like the Phoenix, is coming back to life. It actually flourished nearly a century ago, serving as the cornerstone of most psychological theory. Janet (1907), Prince

(1906), and others felt that human behavior and thought were not determined by some single source, but rather by a variety of sources. Some of these were thought to be fully conscious while others were either co-conscious or not conscious at all. Hypnosis was becoming popular as a psychological treatment; and from these experiences, it was evident that many diverse "states of mind" were possible, as well as clinically useful.

The demise of the concept began, strangely, with the advent of psychoanalysis. Hypnosis fell into disfavor, and the notion of Dissociation was essentially replaced by that of Repression. The real death knell, however, was sounded by the Behaviorists when they convinced the world that if something was not empirically verifiable, it was not worth paying serious attention to. And that was the end for Dissociation because at that point in time we did not know how to demonstrate its existence in the laboratory.

The rebirth began much sooner in the public consciousness than in professional psychology. The popularity of *Sybil* and *Eve* made it apparent that the idea of multiple layers of awareness struck a chord in the lay psyche. Once again, the first professionals to acknowledge it were the practitioners of hypnosis, probably because they witnessed it with such regularity. Gradually, it snuck back into the thinking and writing of many clinicians. As recently as five years ago, there were very few psychiatric hospitals that had established treatment programs for Dissociative Disorders. Today, it is hard to find one that does *not* have such a program! There is at least one professional periodical focusing on the topic (entitled *Dissociation*), and there may well be others in the works.

Coming full circle, it has even made its way back into the laboratory. Psychologists have recently done an impressive series of studies on something they call Implicit Memory. While interpretations of the results vary, the basic idea is that we learn and retain a lot more than we are immediately aware of. Under the right circumstances, we are able to call up this information that we had no idea was in our heads. Meanwhile, neuroscientists are taking seriously the idea that personality can be fractured into numerous parts and are finding that EEG tracings are quite different depending on which personality part is accessed. (See Epilogue.)

This waxing and waning of the concept of Dissociation is curious indeed. How can we have allowed to die something that has such rich potential and that now seems to be opening so many doors into the mind? Social climate obviously has a lot to do with it, but those forces are so complex as to be well beyond the scope of this book. Suffice to note that scientific progress is not a steadily forward-moving thing, but more a series of fits and starts, of insights and obfuscations. Human nature is not ideally suited to science.

CHAPTER V

DREAMS

Among the various sorts of dreams that occur, at least three are important in this sort of therapy:

1. **Strategy Dreams.** These are dreams that are about important events in our current lives, such as impending exams, having surgery, deciding whether to adopt a child, etc. This is when we practice "lucid dreaming." We will try out one story line or one strategy, perhaps find it unacceptable, and then alter it to see how we like the adjusted outcome.

2. **Repressed Trauma Dreams.** These dreams bring to our attention portions of a repressed trauma. These can include feelings of suffocation, or panic, or some piece of what is repressed, as described in Chapter IV.

3. **Dreams About Ego States.** These dreams inform us of the internal changes and struggles that are occurring as the alignment of power among the Ego States shifts during therapy.

Let's consider some examples of each.

STRATEGY DREAMS

Paul had a dream that he had an important physics exam the following day, but overslept and as a result failed the course. One of the things we knew about him was that he had a tendency to self-destruct at certain points in his life. He was exceptionally bright and had the capacity to be a top-level student. But because of things that we were learning about his early life, we also knew that he carried a deep sense of shame and worthlessness. Because of this, he would occasionally place his right foot directly in front of his left and fall on his face. On the ground face-down felt like where he really belonged.

He had done very well in the physics course up to this point, but the final exam constituted half the course grade. Failing it would mean not being able to graduate and probably derail his hopes of getting into a graduate program. Thus we took the dream as a warning. We used it as a means of discussing the practical consequences of various courses of action and formulated a plan.

In trance, I talked to the Ego State which was known to be the source of the self-derailment. I asked if we could strike a deal. The deal was that he allow Paul to go ahead and take the exam on time in exchange for the promise that he (the Ego State) would be granted extra time during the next month to talk about himself. This he found acceptable, and Paul passed the exam and the course with high marks.

My thinking here was that the exam had important consequences for the remainder of Paul's life and that this Ego State was not yet mature enough to appreciate this fact. I hoped that in time, as the sense of shame receded, all of him would be glad that we had done this. In general, I rarely interfere like this in people's daily lives. The next example will show why.

Joan was a wife, a mother of two adolescents, and a full-time nurse. She was a highly responsible person who could be counted on by everyone she dealt with. However, she found it hard to take care of herself or her own needs.

During therapy, we accessed a Part called Joanie who was quite young and who liked more than anything to play silly games, just for fun.

At some point, I got the bright idea to invite Joanie to participate more actively in Joan's daily life, so as to offset the drudgery of caring for everyone else but herself. My suggestion was that whenever Joanie sensed that Joan was getting back in the rut of over-responsibility, she should gently shake her arm to remind her of what she was doing. This sounded innocent enough to me (I was still fairly new at this).

The next day I received a phone call from Joan, insisting that I remove this hex forthwith and immediately. What had happened was that Joanie, being young and playful, thought that Joan was being too responsible ALL the time! Thus, Joan's arm had been twitching slightly, but incessantly from the time she had left my office. Joan had thought that it would quit (still finding it hard to believe that it was really happening anyway), and it wasn't that noticeable to anyone else. But it was embarrassing, and 24 hours was more than enough of this!

The moral of this story is: Don't Take Sides. The balance of power among the Parts is so complicated and so constantly shifting that you have no idea what the consequences will be. A short-term gain may turn out to be a long-term debacle and can lead to a loss of trust.

REPRESSED TRAUMA DREAMS

These are the ones that contain some element or clue as to the nature of a trauma that is beginning to come to awareness. Michelle dreamed about a complicated story that she couldn't remember much of, except for one thing. There was a peculiar pattern of black and grey that ran throughout the dream, and it made her sick.

In trance, I asked the Part that knew about this to tell us more. Nothing happened for several minutes, and we were tempted to abandon this and pursue something else.

Just as we were ready to leave the topic, she saw a bright light. It came and went in an instant. That was all. We noted its occurrence and waited again for more information, but to no avail.

The following week she dreamed about an upstairs bedroom at her aunt's house. The dream wasn't particularly frightening, and there was no obvious portent, but we checked it out anyway. As she visualized the bedroom in more detail, she was surprised at all the things she remembered: the color of the wallpaper, the sheer curtains, even a picture that always hung crooked. Toward the end of the session, she reported a disquieting sensation which made no sense at all: something very cold to the touch, almost like the skin of a snake. We had no idea what this was about, but it was duly noted.

The whole matter seemed to go underground for a couple of weeks until she had another dream. In it, a man with dark eyes and a moustache was leering at her in a way that made her want to run away from him. She ran, but the floor was slick, and her feet went nowhere. The more she tried to run, the more she panicked. She became breathless and awoke screaming. During that session, she cried quietly for no apparent reason, except that she said that she felt very bad.

The following week, she reported that she had remembered the pattern on the floor of the bedroom. It was linoleum (cold to the touch, feels like a snake) and was exactly the same black and grey pattern as in the first dream. She was pacing when she put the two together. Suddenly, she felt so faint that she had to sit down. As she described it, she shook visibly. She then wept and reported the same feeling of badness.

Two weeks later, it came together. In trance, I asked her who came to mind when she thought of dark eyes and a moustache. She was motionless and gasped as though she had seen a ghost. Her body became rigid, and she began to shake. This persisted for about fifteen minutes and was interspersed with shouts of "I don't WANT to do that!" and

"Let me go! I want to go be with Auntie!"

Her uncle had introduced her forcibly to the world of petting at a much-too-young age. It had not been physically painful, but she was deeply shamed. There was an overhead light in the bedroom that had no fixture over it, and she had focused on it as a way of escaping the situation. The black and grey pattern was in the linoleum on which they were sitting. Auntie had gone to take a meal to a sick church member and was only gone for a short while. But it was long enough. We never found any reason to believe that this happened more than once. But it, and the threat to make her never tell about it, left an indelible impression.

The cycle of dreams relating to this event covered about eight weeks. During that period, we were never sure about the clues we were seeing, or whether they were clues at all. What usually makes it even more complicated is that the mind does not deal with just one incident at a time. Sometimes it will present us with a thread that is common to two or three events, and then jump back and forth from one to the other helter-skelter. All we can do is take seriously the material that is presented and wait for it to make sense when we finally have enough pieces of the puzzle to see what is being depicted.

DREAMS ABOUT EGO STATES

Mary dreamed that a man, woman, and child were pursuing her and that she was having to physically beat them off. She somehow got the woman down on the floor, but the woman kept twisting her head to make Mary look at her face. The faces of all three — a family — were extremely ugly, with skin hanging loosely around their cheeks. Otherwise, their bodies seemed normal. She wasn't sure whether she killed the woman, but she definitely wanted to.

Mary had come to therapy with the conviction that her family life had been fine. Her reason for coming was that she couldn't get along very well with people and wanted to work on that. In time, she discovered that there was a connection — that her family life had something to do with her lack of friends.

This dream was the first occasion on which we were allowed to see three basic Ego States. They represented the bad things about her mother, her father, and herself as a child. They were all things she had spent her life refusing to see. That is why in the dream the mother is trying to force Mary to look at her face: she wants to be acknowledged, to finally be recognized and remembered. Mary, in turn, wants to kill her.

The reason for the loose skin was that her parents were obese. Even though she never was, she always felt she must be, by kinship. In fact, she became nearly anorexic for a time to protect against that body image. The dream message was: "Here we are. It's about time you faced us." This is one of the ways that Ego States are most often introduced. They are portrayed as forcing themselves into the person's perceptual field in some way. Usually the person responds much as Mary did, by trying to kill them or at least drive them away.

Many dreams similarly depict the person being "assaulted" or "attacked" by monsters or ugly creatures who turn out to represent something that the person has never felt, or faced, within themselves. An adolescent in treatment used to dream of being chased by huge, terrible monsters through big-city streets in which there were no people. He would wake up in a horror, certain that the monsters meant to kill him. But little by little, he began to realize that they weren't really trying to KILL him, but were just AFTER him for some reason. I encouraged him to try to turn around at some point in one of the dreams and see if he could actually look straight at the monsters (which he never had done).

Once he began doing this, he realized that they were not nearly as big or as menacing as he had assumed. Eventually, they turned out to be representations of his own anger and bitterness, things that were constantly causing him to get into trouble with his family, school, and the law, making his life a misery. All of them were associated with his being beaten severely as a youngster, and the resulting rage, helplessness, and violence that plagued him.

ERRORS IN DREAM INTERPRETATION

One of the things I have learned is to *not* try to interpret someone else's dreams. Instead, I now feel much safer just asking the Part that created it to tell us about it. Let me give an example of how this came about.

One man dreamed of being entirely alone at the beach. There were other people there, but they kept a great distance away. He felt a curious longing for some specific thing, but could not identify what is was. I felt sure I knew what it was. This dream was plainly about existential aloneness, and the thing he longed for was intimacy, etc., etc. Wrong. In trance, one of the Parts gave a totally different account, which both I and the person knew to be correct as soon as we heard it.

This man had a drinking problem. While he was not an alcoholic, he had relied on it much of his life to give him relief from his difficulties. He had recently tried for the first time to give it up. He proudly reported that it was a snap and that he was relieved to find that he wasn't nearly as dependent on it as he had feared. The Ego State that did the talking said that he and a couple of others were really tired of his drinking and the trouble it caused. In the dream, they sent him away to a beach where he had no access to alcohol, and they could watch him from a distance to make sure that he did not sneak away to get it. They wanted him to be by himself so that he could have the opportunity to take a good hard look at himself, possibly for the first time. Sure enough, he immediately experienced the craving for a drink, even though he would not admit it to himself.

The dream was helpful to him in forcing him to face up to his dependency. It was helpful to *me* in getting me to face up to my arrogance. Given the amazing complexity of the mind, it strikes me as arrogant that I would ever have presumed to interpret someone else's dream for them. One of the great advantages of having access to Ego States is being able to ask them directly what the dream is about. Not that they are always able to tell you right at that moment. Sometimes there is too much pain involved, and they can only help by providing further clues. They then allow time for those to be absorbed and subsequently move on to provide greater amounts of information until the real subject matter is fully disclosed.

CHAPTER VI

ENDORPHINES

It will be helpful to understand something about the role of endorphines in order to make sense out of how Alters and Ego States get formed. Endorphines are neurotransmitters, meaning that they act on the electrical signals in the brain. Their effect on the body is similar to that of morphine, in that they act to reduce the awareness of pain. They seem to function like circuit breakers in an electrical system. When the system is overloaded with pain signals (presumably to the point where actual physical damage to the brain could occur), endorphines are automatically secreted, awareness of pain diminishes, and a reasonable electrical balance is restored.

Let's consider the case alluded to above. A soldier steps on a land mine, and it blows off most of one leg. Within seconds, there is so much pain information flooding the brain that it threatens overload. Within just a few more seconds, the brain somehow computes the type of endorphine needed (some are much stronger than others) and the amount. These are immediately released into the brain, and the soldier experiences a sudden sense of relief.

Let's look at two different scenes. First, let's assume that he gets prompt medical attention, the bleeding is stopped, and all that can be done is done. His body may soon recognize that the life-threatening danger is over. This will result in a diminution of alarm and pain signals in the brain, and the endorphines will be reduced proportionately. Once these signals fall below a certain threshold, the endorphines will no longer have to be secreted at all. When that happens, the soldier will come out of his merciful stupor and be flung back into the teeth of pain. The point here is that the proper role of endorphines is to block out of consciousness only that part of the pain that we cannot stand. Once it subsides to a level that is electrically tolerable, the secretions subside, and the pain returns.

Let's now change the picture somewhat. If we imagine that the soldier is alone, or for some reason is not cared for quickly, both the alarm and the pain signals are just going to keep growing in intensity. In that case, the brain is called upon to secrete ever greater amounts and strengths of endorphines to counteract these escalations. If this continues long enough, the soldier may well go into a state of shock. Later, if no help arrives, he may lapse into coma.

The following graph may help to explain this phenomenon.

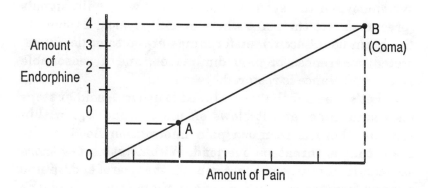

Here, the vertical axis represents the amount of pain, and the horizontal axis the amount of endorphine required to quell the pain. You can see that up to the point of threshold, at A, no endorphines are secreted. Even though the person is in considerable pain just short of A, the body withholds its endorphines until the circuit threatens to blow. After A, it begins an incremental response, meaning that the amount of endorphine is proportional to the amount of pain.

One thing that I must confess immediately is that this entire line of thought hinges on one issue that is not currently resolved. Namely: does the brain respond in the same way to emotional pain as it does to physical pain? This is a pivotal question, and a moment's reflection will tell you why it is not resolved. It is difficult, but not at all impossible, to measure brain response to physical pain. The experimenter need only have access to persons in a hospital Emergency Room, or some such. Blood samples, already drawn, tell us about amount of endorphines in the body and brain.

But what about emotional pain? Where are we going to get people to study? How are we going to create emotional situations in the laboratory intense enough to warrant endorphine secretion? In some countries this might be possible, but in the U.S. there are very strict prohibitions against anything of the sort. So we are left partially in limbo. Some neuroscientists that I have talked with personally have stated that there is no reason to assume that the brain would react any differently to the two sources of pain. But few are willing to go out on that limb in print because of the lack of hard experimental evidence.

Having acknowledged this partially missing piece of the puzzle, I would argue that even if it turns out not to be the endorphines, *something* in the brain serves this very function. The fact that memories of the pain get stored, even though they are not experienced in consciousness at the time, tells us that a repressive process is clearly taking place. And when the brain has a built-in mechanism that works so well for physical pain, it is hard to see why some other — or very different — mechanism would be required for emotional pain. Let's proceed then, on the assumption that the endorphines actually do provide the mechanism of action and see what it means for psychological repression.

First of all, there need be no repression of mildly

painful experiences (anything to the left of point A in the graph). We might well have a stored memory of the experience, but it will be readily available to consciousness. But what happens *after* A? Where do these repressed experiences get stored in the brain, and why are they so hard to get at?

Let's take an example just to the right of A. Susan's grandmother dies unexpectedly. The two had been very close. Susan is only five, and the idea of death is quite new and frightening. Her parents notice that she does not cry at the funeral and that she seems to have a vacant stare. She is in a mild state of emotional shock and is only partially "awake" to the experience. It is weeks later before it really hits her. She has several nightmares. Her parents can see that the fears relate to her grandmother's death, and they let her talk and cry it out. (Lucky girl!) Shortly, she is "herself" again.

This phenomenon is familiar to virtually everyone. We often say of intense experience (very good *and* very bad), "It hasn't hit me yet. I'm still in shock." And we know even as we say this that at some point in the future the feelings will come home to roost. Thus, with experiences such as Susan's, the degree of repression is not too great. The feelings involved may be temporarily repressed for a week or two, but then they come flowing forth quite readily.

But what about serious emotional traumas? These fall increasingly to the right of A in the graph. For intense traumas, we would assume that the amount and/or strength of endorphine response would again be proportional to the amount of emotional pain. Thus, in very severe cases, the state of "shock" might last for many hours, and possibly even days. Then when the person is fully "awake" again, the memory is either completely gone or well along the way to full repression. Unfortunately, I can't be more specific. HOW this process occurs is still mostly a mystery. But judging from clinical experience, this is what seems to happen.

CHAPTER VII

SEXUAL ABUSE

"If only there were evil people somewhere insidiously committing evil deeds, and it were necessary only to separate them from the rest of us and destroy them. But the line dividing good and evil cuts through the heart of every human being. And who is willing to destroy a piece of his own heart?"

— From the *Gulag Archipelago*
(Solzhenitsyn, 1973)

There is something about sexual abuse of children and adolescents that seems to predispose them particularly to processes of dissociation, and thus to Ego State Disorder. For reasons that I do not fully understand, it is a uniquely powerful kind of trauma. Even in cases where a parent has not done anything to physically hurt the child (e.g., petting, masturbation), there is nonetheless a feeling on the part of the child of being sorely wounded and viscerally sickened, far beyond what we might have expected. They seem to experience it as *themselves* having violated the most basic of social rules, of having committed a sin so grievous that they can never again be washed clean.

I have personally been surprised to see this reaction even in children who are preverbal — twelve to sixteen months of age. It is as though the reaction is instinctual and has little or nothing to do with "learning" about social taboos. Somehow they have this gut reaction long before they could possibly have incorporated these sorts of social constraints in any cognitive or verbal way.

There has been ongoing debate within psychology for decades as to whether we are born with certain kinds of knowledge, tendencies, or instincts accumulated by our ancestors (sometimes called "genetic memory"). For example, are so many people afraid of snakes because there was a period in human history when snakes were prevalent enough and poisonous enough to pose a daily threat to human existence? Will this fear drop out after some thousands of years of NOT having to worry about snakes? The issue is far from settled, but the matter of profound reaction to sexual abuse has made many clinicians wonder whether we might be born with a revulsion to it, that there might be a "feeling in our bones" that tells us how wrong it is.

AN EXAMPLE

I offer the following brief case discussion because it illustrates how easily this travesty can occur. I am not trying to make parents more phobic about this whole business than they probably already are. But I also know well the power of denial, and how strongly inclined we are to assume that this always happens "to someone else."

Helen was four when it happened. They were on vacation, and her mother had taken her older sister shopping — just down the street. Helen was supposed to stay behind and take a nap because she had been rowdy all morning, and besides her dad wanted to rest a while. He was on the bed in just his boxer shorts and insisted that she get in with him. She wasn't the least bit sleepy, so what is there to do lying in bed? As she had done many times before, she started crawling her fingers across his tummy, pretending that she would fall into a pool — his belly button. Always before he had played along and pretended to rescue her in dramatic fashion.

But this time he pointed out to her that her crawling

fingers made his "peepee" rise and fall. He made her look at it while he made it move at will. She didn't want to look, but it *was* kind of fascinating. Then he suggested that it would rise and fall even more if she would touch it directly. The strangest feelings washed over her. She felt sick, she wanted to run, she felt nasty. And what made it so much worse was that she also felt sexually aroused. Not much, but enough to intensify her confusion tenfold. When she refused, he said that she must at least take off all her clothes so he could see *her* peepee. With great shame, she did it, and then held both hands between her legs. He pushed her hands away and shoved his arm beneath her so that it rubbed her bottom.

That was "all" — at least for the time being. Soon after, her mother and sister returned, and it seemed like everything was back to normal. But it turned out to be just the beginning. She lived the next eight or ten years feeling like she was incessantly being hunted down by him. He allowed her no privacy at all, and the abuse got much worse. If he was anywhere around, she found herself tied up in chronic muscular tension. He of course knew exactly how to ensure that she never told anyone . . . until almost thirty years later. A long time to keep a deadly secret.

What is so striking to me about this story, and that of many other persons, is how "innocently" it begins. It is a hot summer day, and a grown man is left alone with a sweet young girl. She does what any young girl would do, and yet somehow it leads to this terrible unforeseen conclusion. In saying this, I am *not* trying to excuse the abuse. There is in the final analysis no excuse for what he did, and he must be held completely morally and legally accountable. But it all happened so quickly! Did he even intend for it to happen? I doubt that in most cases the first occurrence is planned at all. Many abusers are probably later shocked at their own behavior. Some of them are, enough so that it never happens again.

SEXUAL ABUSE AND DISSOCIATION

However innocently it might begin, sexual abuse is traumatic enough in most instances that it requires of the child an extreme defensive posture — namely, making herself go elsewhere in her mind: dissociating. At first blush, this doesn't seem so bad. Most children, after all, spend a fair amount of time in fantasy, daydreaming and the like. What makes the dissociation of sexual abuse so much more worrisome is both the frequency and the intensity of the process. The more often the abuse takes place, the more habituated dissociation becomes as an escape from any form of unpleasantness or anxiety.

Adult "survivors" of abuse often describe themselves as lazy and indifferent because they have become so accustomed to running from distress into fantasy, and thus into inactivity and lethargy. (In reality, it often turns out that others do not perceive them this way, but this is the way they *feel*.) The intensity of the dissociation is also a problem in that as the abuse persists, the child learns to go away farther, faster, and to stay away longer. All three of these things are true of the habit patterns thus formed.

It is easy to see how these periods of being "gone" would also make the child's life a lot harder in school and later at work and in relationships. These people, as adults, find themselves standing with someone, obviously having a "conversation," but being so far gone that they have no idea what has been said for the last five or ten minutes. They are able to nod their heads more or less appropriately, but they are a million miles away. When they wander back "in," they have to deal with the fear that they will be asked to respond, in which case the jig will be up. True, everyone does this to some extent with really boring conversation. Again, the difference is one of degree. ESD people have very little control over when and to what extent it happens. And that is a serious social liability.

I have been struck with the "ingenuity" that children show in their dissociative responses. One woman learned to

concentrate so hard on her ears that she could actually hear
the blood flowing in and around them. She had no idea that
she had ever done this until one day when some bad memories started rushing back. Suddenly there it was, the same
strange sound that had provided so much comfort to her as
a child, offering relief to her as an adult. As a child, she
never questioned it; she was simply grateful for it. As an
adult, she could question the nature of it and discern the
actual cause.

Some children learn to distort the shape of their eye-
balls in order not to see what they are having to witness. If
they have to, they can then begin to pay close attention to
all the strange shapes and colors that result from this dis-
tortion as well as the physical pain in the area of the eyes. (I
wonder whether this might contribute to far- or near-sight-
edness and to astigmatism. Many of these people have to
wear glasses.) Later on, they may have chronic or occa-
sional pain in that area that seems to have no physical basis.

Sexual abuse can lead to other strange symptoms. One
person, for as long as he could remember, hated Sundays.
He also hated going to church, not because he was against
religion but for some unspecified reason that he could never
explain. As it turned out, his abuse had typically occurred
on a Sunday. The reason was because that was the only day
he was left alone with the perpetrator — everyone else had
gone to church. Occasionally, he would have to go on to
church afterward and to pretend that nothing had happened. Small wonder he hated it.

In the course of treatment, people often discover odd
things about their sexual tastes and habits that derive from
the abuse. Masochistic rituals often have their roots in
painful molestation. Some people have a morbid fear of
being touched in certain areas of their bodies while the rest
of their sex life seems relatively normal. In general, I have
learned to expect these people to have a diminished libido,
at least prior to treatment. They nearly all report that they
don't really enjoy sex that much and not as much as their

friends do. One of the best indications I have that they are getting better is when their sexual appetite improves. I realize that if ever there was a clinical cliché, that's it. But it seems to be true for these people.

I think that there is another important side effect of molestation that is not commonly acknowledged, one that is much more true for girls than boys. Some of the young girls who are abused seem to quickly learn that they wield considerable power through sex. Once they become aware that they are valued as a sexual object, their self-esteem becomes intimately tied to their sexuality. This is all the more true because of the fact that their self-esteem has been otherwise so badly shattered.

Unfortunately (for the long run), they are able to take some satisfaction in exploiting this power. A teenage girl who is openly sexual is awarded instantaneous popularity — at least among the males. Young boys (of many ages) find this nearly irresistible and fall over themselves trying to compete for these girls' attentions, especially their sexual favors. This fact is not lost on the girls themselves. They eventually come to enjoy being able to dangle and maneuver the boys like so many puppets. The boys are convinced that it is sex the girls are after. Hardly. The sex itself is an afterthought and something that is usually enjoyed little or not at all. It is the sense of power that drives them and possibly the sweet taste of revenge. They get to control and thereby make a fool out of the gender that did it to them. Again, one of the surest signs that a woman is benefiting from therapy is when she is able to give up this kind of power and control.

I do not mean to portray these women as sexual powermongers. It is not as though they have adopted this position willfully. It is instead something that has been forced upon them and a behavioral pattern that they carry out robotlike. There is very little real satisfaction in it, sexual or otherwise. But some power is better than none at all. When they were originally abused, they were stripped of any sense of personal power that they may have had, partly because of the deep shame and partly because of the feelings of total helplessness that ensued. So when they find years later that boys are drawn to them like bees to honey, it is nearly impossible to not capitalize on that awakening. I think it is something that can only be surrendered when the woman finds empowerment within herself in forms that are more fundamentally satisfying.

Not all women who are abused display this behavior, but many do. The reason that it is not true for men is quite simple. Can you imagine a teenage *boy* letting it be known that he is sexually available? Who cares? Which one isn't? So there is no exceptional power granted him, and the developmental pattern is quite different. What *does* happen with many abused boys is that they become preoccupied with sex altogether. There is often an equation in their minds: Sex equals Love. This is a very difficult pattern to break and an excellent sign for therapy when it finally starts to happen.

There has been a lot of attention paid recently to what is called "sexual addiction." It seems to be increasingly prevalent among both men and women. For many of these people, sex is not something they do so frequently because it feels wonderful or because they so much enjoy sharing the dance with a special person. Rather it is more like a compulsion — something they *must* do often in order to avoid a terrible feeling that arises otherwise. If the preceding discussion is correct, I would expect to find sexual abuse at the heart of the matter for many of the "addicts."

It seems that we as a society are beginning to acknowledge the horrible price we pay for allowing adults to use children for sexual purposes. Presumably, this has been going on for untold generations. But it has been cloaked in the darkest secrecy. There is considerable reason to believe that Sigmund Freud was aware of the problem almost a century ago. By 1896, he was convinced that molestation of children was one of the primary causes of adult neurosis. But after about a year of being ridiculed and slandered for this opinion (this was an age of intense sexual repression), he recanted. He decided that what was being reported to him were not actual events, but the contents of either dreams or fantasies.

But as Schultz (1990) observes, "It must be noted that Freud never denied that the childhood sexual abuses his patients reported might have occurred. What he did deny was his earlier view that they had *always* occurred. 'Such widespread perversions against children are not very probable,' Freud wrote (Freud, 1985, p. 264)." Apparently, the tip of the iceberg had been sighted and then quickly discounted. It has taken nearly one hundred years for us to run solidly aground on it.

I wonder if the current media exposure of sexual abuse might potentially have some considerable value. When I see the way it ruins people's lives, and the way this has continued for so many years, I wonder if it is not one of the greatest dangers we face. But if we can somehow face it squarely, not turn away from it, maybe we can improve our lot as humans. I have no idea how we are to deal with it, but almost anything at this point is better than nothing. At least once we start trying things, we will learn from our mistakes.

My worst fear is that the whole matter will go underground again. There are so many forces in our society and in each of us individually that make us want to close our eyes and ears to this. It is so ugly, so sickening, that we too find ourselves wanting to dissociate. I hope we have the strength not to.

I also think that this openness to the reality of abuse may prove to be very helpful in psychotherapy. I can recall, many years ago, working intensively with people over a long period of time, and so often having the nagging feeling that something was missing. The puzzles still had a hole in them. In many cases, sexual abuse was the missing piece, and always a *big* piece. I know that now. I wish I had known it then.

One final note: perpetrators are not inhuman. They are all too human. (In many cases, they have been abused themselves. I doubt that any pedophile was born into this life with a sexual preference for children. Something very bad had to have happened to them.) One of our first dissociations is *from them*. That is a mistake. If we cannot see that, under the right circumstances, given enough of our own horror, we would do much the same thing, then we should probably stay out of the fray.

A patient recently wrote this poem, which says a lot:

I'll sue you in a court of law.
I'll tell them what you did,
How you touched and fondled me
When I was just a kid.

I'll raise my hand and take the oath
And swear that I won't lie.
Then I'll take the witness stand
And start to testify.

I'll tell them first about your games —
How you made your penis wiggle,
And how to buy a little time,
I'd stare at it and giggle.

I'll tell them how your eyes were glazed,
How you'd lick your lips and smile.
I'll duplicate the way it looks
To molest a little child.

Then I'll tell them how it felt
When suddenly I knew
That you were doing something
That a decent Dad wouldn't do.

I'll show them how I closed my eyes
And hung my head in shame,
And how, because it felt good,
I took on all your blame.

Then I'll repeat the scary threats —
You told me I was bad.
You told me I would go to jail
For what I did to Dad.

I'll tell them how I cried at night,
Of how my heart was broken.
I'll pour out all the secrets
That I've never ever spoken.

I'll tell them how you could have been
The best dad in the world
If only you had treated me
Like a precious little girl.

When I have told them everything
I'll simply rest my case.
I'll leave you stripped before them
With guilt upon your face.

I'll smile as you sit — beaten —
Before the angry crowd.
And when the judge says guilty,
You'll hear me laugh out loud.

I'll dance as they haul you away
To lock you in that cell
And know when you next leave it —
You'll find yourself in Hell.

CHAPTER VIII

IMAGES AND METAPHORS

I said earlier that it would be helpful for the reader to approach this material more from an intuitive than a rational standpoint. I find myself doing exactly that within the context of psychotherapy. Not that I never do any rational mental operations. Of course I do. But I find that overall my thinking is very much guided by a number of images and metaphors that I have come to trust. Some are transient and have only to do with a certain moment in time or a set of feelings having to do with a single event. Others are more enduring. Among them:

RESONANCE

Imagine two violins tuned exactly alike, lying side by side. If you pluck any of the strings on one instrument, it will cause the corresponding string on the other to vibrate — less strongly, but quite audibly. This is very similar to what happens when the therapist is able to "tune in" to what a patient is saying. The intensity of reaction is never quite as strong, but it is essentially parallel.

When this occurs, the patient senses the empathy and the accompaniment and is likely to feel several things. First, there is a sense of being validated. If someone else feels the same thing, then I am not completely alone. Second, his reacting that way shows me that I am not crazy — that these events really do lead to these feelings, even for him. Third, there is a domain of safety that is created. Knowing that someone is paying close attention *and* understanding what I say makes me able to go further. I have a lot more courage to dive into that dark, murky water if I can feel sure that he is close by.

I think this image applies not just to therapy generally, but also to hypnosis. It is possible to hypnotize people by using gimmicks, by surprising them with some unexpected induction that creates a temporarily "altered state of mind." But this only works a time or two. People don't like to be tricked, even if they think it is for their own good. In the long run, it is better to describe to the patient exactly what you have in mind and to ask if they want to try it. Trust is not only preserved, but reinforced.

DIVIDE AND CONQUER

Think back to Bob for a moment. When Mom had to suppress all the other Ego States, she also had to keep them separated. Together they would have made life miserable for her, and for Bob. If they had been able to unite, they would have posed a much more powerful threat to her control. The Knower would have told the Child all about the dark side of the real mother and would have had all the energy of Sport and the ingenuity of the Mason to assist him. There would have been no denying them access to consciousness. Mom knew that (probably from the experience of actually having it happen) and had to ensure that it did not occur.

So when she locked them away, it was in separate vaults. (These are variously described by patients as "cells," "cubby holes," "caves," and even "mummies.") One day perhaps we will understand how this separation is accomplished, but not today. We can, in the meantime, simply relate what is described to us.

One of the detrimental effects of this separation is that the development of each Ego State is stunted. Each has its own highly idiosyncratic way of perceiving the world and filters incoming information through the same perceptual mesh day after day, without much opportunity for revision. If the States had access to each other, there could be a sharing and a comparison of points of view. This would benefit everyone, including the primary person.

Unfortunately, that is not what happens. Instead, each one locked away in its own compartment has only its same old rigid attitudes and biases to guide it. It learns very little through the accumulation of experience because everything "new" is seen in the same old ways. For that reason, when Ego States are first contacted, they often seem retarded or naive. Once they are out, they learn and mature rather quickly. But they are always resentful at having had to spend so much time "in the dark."

THE ONION

The unconscious resembles an onion in the sense that there are many, many layers to it and that access to the next one underneath is naturally accorded by removing the one on top. As mentioned above, I think that the layering depends on the amount of pain involved. Outermost layers, the ones that are first encountered in therapy, are usually the least painful of the repressed memories. And so on, down to the most painful of all at the core.

Yes, it is possible to penetrate more deeply, more quickly, as with a knife into an onion. In therapy, the equivalent is with an intrusive form of hypnosis, with LSD, or sodium pentathol. But there is a price to pay for the greater speed: somewhere in the unconscious, a huge steel door shuts ever so quietly. We don't hear it, but we find out later that we have created a nearly immovable obstacle. The point about taking the onion skins off gradually, and in their natural order, is that it allows time for *accommodation* to take place. Every unpeeling is painful to the person, and the whole system needs time to absorb all the changes that take place.

There are many different facets to any one experience. These things have to be felt individually. One thing might take a week, and the tougher ones might take months to fester out completely. Trying to do this too quickly tends to make people suicidal and/or briefly psychotic. It also makes them feel that they are failures in the therapy process.

POISONS

Somehow, the accumulation of repressed pains becomes poisonous to the body and to the psyche. It is as though the overload that is stored in the brain is "foreign matter" — something that needs to be expelled in order for the body to regain its healthy balanced state. Just like a thorn in the palm, this composite of memory-and-sensation can't be contained peaceably in the mind. It has to be gotten out. There can be no quiet, no real contentment, until the thorn is gone. While these things are trapped inside the mind, they seem to cause chronic muscular tension and even organ damage over long periods of time. Ulcers, high blood pressure, and asthma are among the maladies that can result.

TIME CAPSULE

Every so often, scientists place a Time Capsule in a location where it is reasonably immune to destruction. It is made of the most durable possible material and is designed to last for thousands of years. It contains evidence of what life is like at this point in time. It is intended to convey that information to future generations or to extraterrestrial visitors in the event we eliminate ourselves from the planet.

When excessively painful events are stored in the unconscious, they are similarly preserved with an uncanny degree of completeness and accuracy and permanence. It is almost as though the system at large recognizes the importance of what has happened and knows that in order to provide for subsequent healing, a complete accounting is required. Strange things get stored: colors, smells, tactile sensations, shapes, twinges . . . things that seem on the surface to be whimsical, but that prove to be essential pieces of the puzzle.

Another peculiar thing is that, when the experience is finally felt for the first time, there is a powerful sense of déjà vu. It is as though in some obscure, indefinable way we knew all along that we had stored that material. We didn't know what it was in any specific way, but we had a rough idea. Once it is finally, completely out, we know it's right with an elemental certainty that transcends our ordinary sense of doubt and cross-examination. The event is recalled in (all-too-vivid) detail, and we are shocked at the brain's ability to store so much information and still keep it secret.

But both before and after, we are not so sure. Before, when there are not quite enough clues collected, we remain anguished and in the dark. And then, two or three days after the final dawning, we're not so sure again. We may notice that we have begun to feel better in certain ways, that things seem to make a lot more sense, and our bodies are less tense. But the memory has already begun to fade, and we wonder if what we remembered was altogether real.

In a way, this makes perfect sense: Why would we bother to preserve something so painful in a way that would directly resurrect the pain? Why not mercifully put it away in some recessive file where it can't hurt us continually? We now know it's there, and we know how to find it should the need arise. But the damage is undone — as much as it can be — so why not quietly close the file? Apparently, that is what we do.

TRENCH WARFARE

As the different Ego States become increasingly estranged from one another, they also become distrustful and often hostile. (That is what many murder dreams are about — one State trying to get rid of another or expressing its hatred of it.) The final posture is much like trench warfare: Neither State can see the other, nor are they able to really hear each other. Thus there is no exchange of information, nothing that helps them to *understand* each other, as would inevitably occur if they stood face-to-face. All they can do in this position is to lob grenades and mortars at each other, being convinced that the "other" is the enemy.

THE INTERNAL THERAPIST

This image did not come out of my head, but instead derives from the literature on Multiple Personality. In some cases, every Ego State seems to be kept track of by a sort of monitor, which we call the IT or Internal Therapist. The IT serves as mediator (helping to settle squabbles among the States), switchboard operator (deciding who needs to be ascendant in a particular situation), and advisor to the outside therapist. The IT's job is to weigh out the variety of relative needs/fears/prohibitions and decide who is best qualified to carry out the task. Basically, one State is then designated primacy for a given period of time.

During waking hours, of course, the most powerful Ego State is almost always in control. It is only during nondefended times (basically, sleep and dream states) where the IT comes into play — where the various States stand a chance of occupying Center Stage. The procedure seems to be somewhat democratic, and the weighing-out is done with regard to what seems best for the overall good of the whole person.

THE WALL OF FIRE
(or The Valley of the Shadow of Death)

When people are close to recalling a repressed trauma, they sense doom. They feel sick, they shake a lot, and they fear that they will not live through it. It reminds me of what it would feel like to approach a wall of fire. You can see something of how wide it is, but you don't know how deep it is. If you could know for sure that you would make it through without burning alive, it would make it a little easier.

It really does feel like fire. As hard as you try to make yourself approach it, your every fiber resists. No matter how many assurances I give, there is still the terrible fear that this will be the end. All I can do is tell the person that I haven't lost anyone yet and have no reason to believe they will be the first.

Thankfully, once someone finally enters and exits safely out the other side, it gets a little easier. Most people have to do this many times. (Very few of us are blessed with single incidents of repression.) It is never something that anyone can look forward to, but there is an increased sense of confidence that builds upon success. Particularly so when there is palpable improvement in their lives because of having gone through it.

CHAPTER IX

EGO STATES IN LITERATURE AND POETRY

The acid test for the existence of something lies (for some of us) in the question of whether it appears in literature and poetry. If not found there, it must be regarded as suspect at best. In the case of Ego State Disorder, it turns out to have a substantial history in both. In a book called *The Split Self from Goethe to Broch*, Peter Waldeck (1979) lists half a dozen authors and poets from Germany alone who have written about it. He finds a consistent theme:

> "The present split self is quite specific in its definition. The basic pattern remains close to the following: A childhood self (usually seen outwardly as an adult) possesses the ability to love, but is oppressed by paternal influence and is juxtaposed to an adult self who possesses full emancipation from the father but lacks the ability to love. Each self thus possesses what the other needs and lacks what the other has. Both selves strive ambivalently — and only on an underlying level, not in explicit, conscious terms — for unity." (pp.18-19)

At first glance, this sounds somewhat unlike the phenomena I have been describing, for two reasons. First, there is the special emphasis on the influence of the father. All these authors lived in nineteenth-century Germany, when fathers ruled the roost and severe physical discipline was the norm. Thus when it came to squelching some facet of childhood personality, it was usually the father who was the villain. In our age, the squelching is more subtle, is accomplished more by emotional than physical means, and may be done by both parents (probably more the mother, currently).

Second, Waldeck seems to imply a split into only two personality Parts, whereas I have claimed to observe an average of three to six. It turns out that some of the authors actually describe three, four, and even five Parts. So this difference is also not crucial. (One other minor difference has to do with most of the fictional characters being male. All the authors felt strongly that their writing was inevitably autobiographical, and all happened to be male. However, there is no apparent reason why the same thing could not happen to females.)

What is much more striking is the amount of similarity. For all the authors, the essential splitting process occurs during childhood and is always a reaction to trauma. The primary trauma has to do with father condemning some aspect of the child's emotions. Sometimes this has to do with a budding assertiveness, sometimes with a boyish affection for the mother, and sometimes a visible "weakness" on the child's part. In each case, the child must force himself to cease and desist in those behaviors. Eventually, he must even manage to make himself "forget" that he had any such feelings or inclinations.

It is at this point that the actual split takes place. The forbidden assertiveness, affection, weakness, or whatever is finally driven underground, out of awareness, and for all practical purposes out of existence. But, as Jung (1940) notes:

"It is a basic psychological principle that a

part of the psyche split off from consciousness only *appears* to be inactivated, but in reality leads to an *obsession* of the personality, whereby the latter's goal-setting behavior is falsified in the sense of the split-off part. Thus when the childlike condition of the collective soul is repressed to the point of total exclusion, the unconscious content assumes control over the conscious goal-setting, whereby the realization of the latter is inhibited, falsified or even destroyed. Healthy progress only comes into being through the cooperation of both." [My italics.]

This rather difficult passage conveys a critical point: Not only does the repressed feeling, event, or behavior not cease to exist, but it actually now exerts a powerful influence over thought and action via *unconscious* means. We then find ourselves doing, saying, and feeling things that seem to make no sense — things that even seem directly contradictory to what we "intended" or thought we intended. In some sense, it is this feeling of confusion, of contradictory purpose, that is at the very heart of neurosis. It is often how we first sense that something is wrong with us, that something needs fixing.

Another similarity between the authors' and my accounts has to do with the sense of loss of ability to love. In every novel surveyed, the Adult Part is unable to love or be loved. Somehow, when portions of the child personality are banished, they take with them into exile this capacity for loving. Even though the adult body continues to live, and possible even to thrive physically, there is always a numbness and a lack of *joie de vivre*. It is as though life can only be fully experienced when the personality Parts are all reasonably present, consciously acknowledged, and integrated. The more parts we have to banish, and the further from our awareness, the less we feel alive, and the less we are able to love.

One of Schiller's (1953) split characters, Karl,

". . . is torn between the desire to regain love (and, more broadly speaking, a divine gift of life itself) and the compulsion to dissociate himself from Franz (the Adult Part). . . . Amalia (his mother) has given Karl the chance to return to her as the whole son, including the Franz personality. But . . . to accept Amalia's love now would be to reintegrate the self and to take responsibility for all of Franz' monstrousness. Karl must choose between a *larger, (if extreme) compass of human qualities* and his moral integrity." [My italics.]

Once again, there is the fundamental struggle to own all of ourselves — even those parts that appear to be socially undesirable or morally repugnant. This does NOT mean that we have to act on every jealous, hateful, or murderous feeling that we have, but only that we have to FEEL it, to note its existence. What we then actually *do* will be some compromise between the raw feeling itself and our rational and moral compunctions. The more we are split, and the less we are aware of our primitive side, the more our socially acceptable behavior is just plain empty and phony. We are nice just because we are programmed to be nice, not because we actually feel like being nice. We can mimic the vital act of loving for awhile, but it soon collapses of its own weight because of falseness and lack of internal conviction.

I mentioned above that all these authors felt that their work was inevitably autobiographical. And indeed, Waldeck finds evidence in their personal lives that leads quite naturally to the Split Self concept. Goethe, for example, went through a period of his life when he was forced to change his personality quite radically.

He had grown up the darling of Frankfurt, both because of his winning personality and because of family position. But Frankfurt was a very different sort of place than Leipzig, where he longed to be, and finally went. Leipzig was at that time a hotbed of intellect, a place where great writers gathered and grew in stature. Frankfurt had loved and nurtured him, but it was by comparison rural and dull.

When he arrived in Leipzig, Goethe felt like a hayseed in the big city. He bought an entire new wardrobe, practiced putting on urbane airs, and discarded much about himself that was guileless and lovable. He worked at being the cynic and at acerbic repartee. When he later returned to Frankfurt, ". . . it was as a 'castaway,' as one who had barely managed to survive the shock of the larger society. He had barely thrown up defenses, including a marked tendency to melancholy . . . and had as yet no clear idea of how to regain his childhood identity . . ." (p. 37)

It is also significant that there had been an intense struggle between Goethe and his father. The latter had seen Goethe as his "golden boy" and had placed immense pressure on him to achieve intellectual heights unattainable for himself. Because of this, the father's love and devotion came with a steep price. Thus it was that Goethe described, ". . . my eagerness to flee to Leipzig, as though I were breaking out of prison." (p. 36)

There was always the question in his mind: Was he behaving the way he did because it garnered so much love and admiration or was that his real personality? His flight to Leipzig appears to have been partially an attempt to answer that question. The fact that all these changes occasioned his first real experience with melancholy is a reminder of what happens when we eschew basic parts of ourselves. We know that something is missing and that we cannot have peace without it.

Kafka (1946) also wrote about the Split Self, and there was basis in his life as well.

"In his diary Kafka described an event in his life in which he sat on a bench on the Laurenziburg — as in the story — and decided that a normal life, and presumably normal love and happiness, were impossible for him. He designated this event

as a 'Leave-taking . . . from the world of appear-
ances of youth.' Strangely, in his account he shifts
from the first to the third person, as though to
suggest that a change — indeed a loss of — identity took place here." (Waldeck, op. cit.)

I expect that most of us, in the process of growing up,
encounter less severe but similar crises. Even such a common
thing as entrance into elementary school can be a great
shock to the system. If we have not learned certain social
skills and how to sit quietly for extended periods of time, we
can be in for a rude awakening. Losing a parent through
divorce, and having to learn how to survive with a new one,
is extremely common. But it can still be quite traumatic.
For a student from a small town, going away to a big
university can be terrifying. And as it did for Goethe, it
tends to prompt the assumption of many new behaviors and
the dispatching of old standbys. Even if the new ones work
exceedingly well, and are permanently adopted, it is to be
hoped that the old ways will not be forgotten and will still
be acknowledged and available to the person. They are
truly old and dear friends and not something to be discarded.

CHAPTER X

A JOURNEY
OF DISCOVERY

In order to appreciate this chapter fully, you have to travel backward in time with me about six years. And you have to pretend you know nothing about Ego States because that was my state of mind at the time. Before the journey . . .

Some years ago, I met a man who knew a good bit about hypnosis — something that had always intrigued me, but which I had never pursued. He told me about one woman who had been referred to him because of paralysis of both arms. Numerous physical exams had revealed nothing helpful, and she had not benefitted from physical therapy. So he suggested hypnosis.

In trance, the woman worked her way back to a recent tragedy — seeing her son being killed in an automobile accident. Even though it was clear to her that he was dead, she had wanted to hold him in her arms one last time before he was taken away. Because of the gruesome shape he was in, the paramedics had restrained her from doing it. But in trance, the therapist urged her to go ahead and imagine holding him for as long as she wanted. Her grief poured out, and when she "awoke," she had regained the use of both arms.

I didn't doubt this story at all. In nearly two decades of

doing therapy, I had seen similar things. And it did seem possible that hypnosis could be a good tool in such cases. I considered it briefly, and then it passed from my mind. Strangely, a few weeks later during a therapy session, I found myself saying to someone, "What do you think about trying a little hypnosis?"

I no more than got the words out of my mouth than a voice inside my head screamed, "Do WHAT? You don't know the first thing about how to go about it!"

As luck would have it, the patient (apparently having not heard the screaming) said, "Sure. Why not?"

Almost immediately, I noticed my heart racing and wondered what in the world was going on. Where had this notion about doing hypnosis come from, how did it sneak out of my mouth, and what was I going to do now?

Actually, I did know a little bit about it. I knew that it had to do with getting relaxed and accessing lower levels of consciousness. So I figured maybe I could wing it. Besides, after so many years of clinical work, I felt like I knew a good deal about the unconscious itself, and that was after all what we would be dealing with. The one glaring thing I *didn't* know was what to say — how to start — those magical words you are supposed to use to get the incantation going. So before the next session I went to the library to find some books on technique. And by the time it rolled around, I had worked up a little verbal hocus-pocus: "Close your eyes. Imagine you're going slowly down some steps . . . down . . . down." Something like that.

I droned on for about five minutes, much more attentive to my own nervousness than to whatever was happening to the patient. However, at some point it dawned on me that she was lying very still, and her breathing was unusually rhythmic and relaxed. I knew that we had gotten over the first hurdle. The trouble was, I hadn't thought about what to do next! I didn't really think I could "hypnotize" anyone, and so I hadn't bothered to think about what happens after the induction!

She seemed quite content to just lie there for awhile,

and it gave me time to come up with another idea. So I suggested that she look for an image that would describe something about her life at this point in time — a picture that would sum up something of how she was doing and feeling. To my surprise, she did it quite easily. We pursued the image and its implications for fifteen minutes or so, and that seemed productive.

But something much more intriguing was happening simultaneously with this: As she was talking, her right index finger was twitching. I had worked with this woman for more than a hundred hours prior to this and had never seen any of her fingers twitch. The more curious fact was that the twitching seemed to occur only at certain points — namely, when I would ask her a question.

By this time, I was probably a little caught up in the "mystique" of actually having hypnotized somebody and allowed my thoughts to travel a course that would have ordinarily seemed bizarre. I asked her if she was aware of the twitching, and she said no. I then asked if she would mind my "trying something." She shuddered slightly and said no. I then spoke directly to the finger that was doing the twitching. I asked if it wanted to respond to the questions also. It twitched.

At that point, it was I that shuddered slightly. I then suggested a code, since the finger couldn't actually speak: A twitch would mean that the answer to a question was yes; no movement would mean no or that it didn't want to answer. I then went over many of the same questions we had just covered about her feelings about her life. This time the answers were different. Not only were they different, but they were also more believable. In general, the responses indicated more depression, more despair, and more anger, all of which fit better with what I knew about her history.

By this time, I was over my nervousness. But now I was thoroughly confused and even a little scared. Whom was I talking to? Rather, who were THEY that I was talking to? Or was this all a fabrication — just some freaky altered mental state? Being afraid to push any farther into this confusion, I brought her out of the trance so we could talk about what was happening. I immediately asked her if she was controlling the finger, secretly hoping she would say yes.

She said no. She was visibly shaken. She said that she was fully awake during the proceedings and was utterly stunned when she felt the finger move by itself. It seemed disconnected from her will, like it had a mind of its own. She also observed that its answers to the questions seemed quite truthful, sort of the way she felt at a much deeper level, but was unable to admit because it was so painful.

I was really relieved to hear this. Now it seemed to me that I could explain the whole thing. We had simply accessed a lower level of her consciousness. One that could, for whatever reason, be more honest about her deeper feelings.

Soon after, I used a similar technique with a few other patients — always with interesting results. They seemed able to enter more deeply into themselves, into their experiences and feelings, than ordinarily. I was beginning to feel that I was learning something really useful, and that this was a tool that might to some degree speed up psychotherapy — usually so painfully slow. So it would be only natural that I would get more training in hypnosis and begin to use it regularly, right?

Wrong. Within a month I quit using it at all. I had several well-polished rationalizations to cover me. One was: Now that I realized that there was nothing magical about it, I could use more familiar techniques to accomplish the same thing (and for a while they actually seemed to work fine). And it's better to stick to what is tried and true. Especially since I had no formal training in these black arts. For such excellent and convincing reasons, I quit doing hypnosis for a full year. I never once admitted to myself that I was quitting because I was scared. It wouldn't have made any sense anyway: What was there to be scared OF?

About a year later, I heard myself say to a patient, "Want to try a little hypnosis?" Again, I wanted to retract the words immediately. Again, it was too late. I had done almost no conscious thinking about it and still don't know whose bright idea it was.

This time around, I found myself doing a quite different sort of induction. Rather than "talk" somebody into hypnosis, I described a method of paying close attention to their breathing and then gave them time to do it for themselves.

(If you close your eyes in a relaxed setting and concentrate your attention on your breathing, it brings into sharper focus everything that is going on inside your body. It's a lot like focusing a microscope: You begin to see certain things with greater clarity than before, partly because you are ignoring a variety of other things that are extraneous to your purpose. One of the other things that you can notice is your heartbeat. Little by little, you can begin to feel every single beat and sometimes even the "pulsing" sensation in your fingertips and temples. For some reason, tuning in to this physical self is a big help in accessing emotions. Quite possibly there is a shift that takes place in the brain itself: People walk through the door at the beginning of a session operating primarily on the dominant, logical side of their brain, and this procedure perhaps helps them to shift their consciousness more toward the feeling-intuitive side.)

Once again, the results were intriguing. I became so convinced of its value that I encouraged all my patients to try it, and most of them began using it for a part of nearly every session.

Soon, however, something else alarming began to happen. I once again "found myself" speaking directly to various characters portrayed in their dreams. If that doesn't sound strange enough, these characters started answering me back! On some occasions, the voice that was answering was quite different from the patient's usual voice. It might sound considerably younger, or softer, or more masculine, or more confident, etc. Fortunately, I had worked with Multiple Personalities and was prepared to some degree for this. Still, it is always shocking to hear a new voice coming out of a mouth that you thought you knew so well. In my own mind, I began calling these various personality segments "Parts."

Meantime, I was getting very nervous, again. None of the psychologists I knew and talked with had had experiences with personality Parts in these ways. It wasn't in any of the textbooks I had studied in graduate school, and I couldn't find anything similar in the scientific literature, despite extensive searching. Now, if the sky looks cloudy to you, and twenty other trained professionals tell you it's perfectly clear, what are you to think? How could you presume that you alone are seeing something that a lot of other fully competent people are missing? I felt very isolated and more than a little bit foolish.

To make matters worse, I knew myself to be capable of a perverse sort of independence: I routinely doubted almost everything. If I couldn't prove it to myself in my own way, then I was very hesitant to take it seriously. In fact, in many ways it made me a slow learner. I was so reluctant to take someone else's word for something (as in reading directions, for example) that I often made silly mistakes that a less skeptical person would have easily avoided. However, it did seem that whatever was learned in this way stayed with me.

Except it this case. This subject matter was so slippery and so difficult to describe or to explain that I often lost confidence in it altogether. I went through many months being quite sure that I was entirely wrong and that I should stop forcing it on unsuspecting patients. I wrote hundreds of pages of notes, not with the intention of writing a book, but just to help me understand this puzzling phenomenon that would not leave me alone. I was confused, frustrated, and sometimes even angry. Angry at the world for giving me no affirmation. But much more angry at myself for being unable to abandon this eccentric point of view.

Then one day an acquaintance loaned me a tape on hypnosis. The title said something about "Ego States," which I had never heard of. But I had been told that it contained something about hypnosis, so I played it. As I listened to someone named Dr. Watkins describe the theory behind this, my heart started racing. It sounded like it had some similarity to what I had been seeing! Then he hypnotized a college student. Presently, a different Part of the student introduced itself in a slightly different voice as "The Old One," saying that it provided a stabilizing influence in his life! I squealed! I ran inside shouting to my wife that maybe I wasn't crazy after all, that maybe this phenomenon was real!

I couldn't rest until I had the phone numbers of these people: John and Helen Watkins, a married couple. I talked to both of them the same day and spent two days attending their workshop a couple of months later on Ego States. Sure enough, their experiences paralleled mine almost exactly. And they had been at it for nearly fifteen years! (They credit the original discovery to Paul Federn [1952].) They had written several articles about it, and as I read them I felt that someone had been reading my mind.

Since then, I have talked to a few other people who have found something, usually also on their own, about Ego States, but precious few. One thing that I hope might come out of writing this book will be the convening of people who know something about it and are interested in getting together to talk about it. I'm confident that there are any number of clinicians out there who are finding the same thing and who have developed their own techniques for understanding and working with it. Putting our heads together should be exciting and productive.

One other question which derived from this experience still haunted me: If Ego States are a reality, and if so many people fall into this category, why is it that there is so little written about it? Over time, I think I have come to some understanding of why this is. First, I don't think there is a clinical training program anywhere that teaches students about this disorder. If students have never heard of it, how would they know to look for it? And why would they have any interest in looking for it if they had no idea what to do if they found it?

When I try to teach someone to flyfish for trout, I often

point out the fish in the water. Only rarely do they see the fish I am pointing at because the image is very subtle. The trout's coloring blends in with the bottom of the stream, and there are only very slight movements of the fins and tail to notice. Once you have seen a few hundred of them, you can find them even in fast-moving riffles. But I often forget that to the untrained eye they are nearly invisible. I think the same is true of both Multiple Personality and Ego State Disorders. They are not obvious at all, and you have to have some idea of what you are looking for in order to see them.

But there may be a more personal reason that we do not see these things also. Fear. It might partly be fear of the unknown and unfamiliar and partly the fear that it may be *all too* familiar and too close to home. I think I experienced both kinds of fear in my own learning process. I really didn't want to see what I was seeing. It was a lot of work. It meant drastically revising my ideas about a lot of things, and I already had more than enough to think about as it was. I don't believe any of us want to change our ways of thinking. We resist it in a variety of clever ways and only succumb if we simply have to.

When Neils Bohr discovered Quantum Theory in 1908, it irritated him. He had been working on solving a certain physics problem using the math that he had always used, but it wasn't working. He worked on it for a considerable period of time and became despondent at what he thought was his ineptitude. He was confident that he was making a mistake, that he wasn't seeing the forest for the trees. He finally resolved to present the problem at a convention so that people with keener minds could untangle his knot. Lots of other physicists then became similarly vexed and irritated, and it was only gradually that they began to see that there was no knot at all, but in fact the key to looking at atomic structure in a whole different way. Ego States compare to Quantum Mechanics in one way: in showing how we sometimes stumble onto new ways of seeing things almost by accident.

The second, more personal kind of fear may have something to do with seeing reflections of our own personalities in Ego State Disorder. I don't think we would find any amount of likeness to be very comforting. In the process of writing this book, I became aware of two different tendencies somewhat like conflicting Ego States of my own. One tended to write in a style that was arrogant and almost belligerent. The basic message seemed to be: "I don't give a damn if you believe it or not. I'm going to tell it like I see it, and I am totally confident it's true." Given the frustrating journey I had been on, the isolation, and my own uncertainties, I can easily see where this attitude would come from.

The other style was quite different: timid, deferential, and apologetic. It tended to write in a way that seemed self-abnegating and confused. Once again, I think I can see why. These are definitely among the feelings that I have experienced. It certainly made the writing more effortful, however! I would write one way, then the other, and then have to revise again in order to strike some middle ground between the two extremes. But I was not pleased to note these opposing states of mind.

I'm not saying that everyone has Ego State Disorder. I don't believe that. But we do have vicissitudes of mood, attitude, and perceptual style which are unsettling to us. Life would be much easier for us if we were more constant in all these domains. The variability means a lot of mental work to keep up with it and having to balance and strive for a reasonable average, or middle ground, that is workable in daily life.

The most basic element of fear may come down to this: waking up one morning to discover that a Part of us had gotten up during the night, taken a pair of scissors, and cut to shreds every piece of clothing we owned. This is precisely the kind of nightmare that Multiples have to live with. In a much more subtle way, I think we all fear getting out of control and having some subterranean part of ourselves take over and do great damage to our lives and our reputations. This fear, to whatever extent each of us disowns it, makes us want to put as much distance as possible between ourselves and the idea of Alters or Ego States. But I think the willingness to see something of ourselves in it can actually be revelatory. The more so, the closer our own personalities come to actually fitting within the category.

One of the ironies of this "discovery" process for me is that now, much later, it all seems so obvious. We all know that there are *degrees* of every illness. There is not some single entity called "Depression." Instead it occupies a whole range, from none at all to where it is overwhelming. So too for the flu. Likewise for diabetes, Parkinsonism, and AIDS. Why then did we ever assume that there would not be degrees of Multiple Personality? Some extremely severe cases and some so much milder that it would be questionable whether we were really calling a given instance by the right name. Again, I think we are just beginning to grasp what it is all about, and looking for "degrees" of something is surely one of the later forms of inquiry. First we have to verify that it is real at all, and then we can attend to the finer points.

I suppose that the writing of this book in some sense signals the end of the journey. Even though I still have moments of doubt, most of what I have described now feels quite solid to me. I feel extremely fortunate to have gone through it. I only hope that it will yield some useful tools in our effort to better clarify these puzzling and fascinating phenomena.

EPILOGUE

One of the things that experimental psychologists ask of their distant relatives, clinicians, is that they provide them with testable hypotheses. In other words, when therapists make the claim that something exists, the laboratory types want them to specify how it can be proven or disproven experimentally. That seems to me a reasonable request, and I want to propose at least two methods by which I think the existence of Ego States can be partially tested.

First, it should be possible to administer a battery of psychological tests to differing Ego States. By testing the States separately, we should see some substantial and consistent differences among the results. These results should reflect what is known or claimed about the nature of the States being tested. Also, an Ego State given an MMPI and a Rorschach should score similarly on each in terms of those features prominent in its personality. The study should be done "blind," meaning that the experimenter is told only the name of the State and nothing about what to expect in terms of personality characteristics.

This may not be easy, however. These States are not as rigid, enduring, or constant as their counterparts, the Alters of Multiple Personality. When they are "present," it is not to the same degree as with Alters, and they are much more easily lost. They do not as forcefully assume the foremost position, to the exclusion of all others. I think they also depend more for their emergence on a sense of trust in the therapist than is true for Alters. This suggests that a therapist familiar with this disorder should administer the tests. It seems to me worth a try. (This procedure, by the way, has been done with Multiples. The results are quite striking and clearly suggest very different psychological profiles for the various Alters.)

Another research tool that has been used with Multiples might be even more decisive for Ego States than psychological testing — namely, the Electroencephalograph, or EEG. Basically, one Alter is called out and asked to perform a few simple mental tasks. From the EEG recording, it is possible to tell something about which areas of the brain are most active and involved in the ongoing thought processes. During succeeding sessions, other Alters are called out and asked to perform tasks of similar difficulty — always one Alter at a time. Although the number of studies is still somewhat limited, some of the results suggest highly significant differences among the Alters (Pitblado, 1982 and 1986; Larmore, 1987; and Putnam, 1982).

The fact that quite different cortical patterns are noted among the various Alters is a powerful piece of evidence. It strongly supports the notion that these Alters are very different psychologically as well. Recently (September, 1992), a patient of mine who has Ego State Disorder asked to have an EEG done to see if the results would reflect some of the differences among his varying Ego States. During the testing, he was able to enter into a good hypnotic trance, and two separate Ego States were elicited for about fifteen minutes each. However, there were no detectable differences among the various States and his normal conscious state. Since other persons will undoubtedly want to pursue this line of research, I offer a few observations that may prove helpful.

First, the EEG is a crude instrument in many ways. Sufficiently so that the experts I talked with prior to testing predicted that we would not find detectable differences. I thought it was worth a try because of two factors: First, one of the Ego States elicited was very young, and there are noticeable differences between EEG's for very young children and adults.

Second, the other Ego State seems to be located mostly in one half of his brain. When this Part is elicited, the patient cries out of only one eye and describes feeling in only one half of his body. Thus, I thought there was a chance that the EEG might pick up some differences in operations of the two halves of the brain. However, it did not.

There are, however, several factors that may account for why nothing was detected. Not only is the EEG crude in some ways, but we also did not have the advantage of computerized averaging across time, which helps to tease out smaller differences. (However, the EEG technician who assisted us is very competent at picking up any abnormalities and was of the opinion that the lesser sensitivity might not have mattered.)

Another factor is that the patient has been in therapy for a good while, and I feel that there has been considerable fusion of his Ego States over time. Even though they are still separately elicitable, all of the Parts know each other quite well, and there has been a great deal of sharing of memories and information among them. Thus, he may have been the wrong person to study — too much dissociation may have been resolved.

A third factor may well be the most important: Although the Parts were elicited, there was very little emotional involvement. In other words, even though we might have been in contact with relatively specific areas of the brain, if they weren't *doing* anything involving much cortical or emotional energy, there would be no reason that the EEG would show any differences. We were in a strange office with a technician whom the patient had never met before, and I did not feel like asking the Ego States any questions that might bring on crying or emotional upset. (Even if this had occurred, the technician's job of *interpreting* the EEG would have become much more difficult. During emotional reaction, it is very difficult to know what the EEG is showing because of muscular involvement, physical movement, etc. All these varying signals have the effect of blurring the picture so that it is very hard to know what is causing what.) It may turn out that a *moderate* amount of emotion might prove more revealing about which parts of the brain were involved, but it would probably need to stay below the level of sobbing or much physical movement.

I have given this account of an experimental failure because I think it is important to do so. Most professional journals only print successes. But this procedure will surely be attempted by others, and they need to know what did not work so that they can avoid some of the pitfalls that we encountered. I still believe it is possible that, given someone with Ego State Disorder who is relatively new to therapy, and a moderate level of emotional arousal during testing, an EEG might display evidence of the differing cortical processes that I feel sure are occurring.

If it turns out to be possible to get a rough measure of "degree of dissociation" in this way, it could provide psychotherapists with something they have longed for forever: a reliable means of assessing and documenting progress in therapy. In other words, if we can perform EEG's as soon as Ego States are identified, and then do yearly follow-ups, we should (if therapy is going well) be able to see the dissociation diminishing. This would be evidenced by EEG's for the various Ego States becoming more like each other as well as more like the person's normal conscious state.

QUESTIONNAIRE

1. Do you sometimes find yourself "zoning out" in the middle of a conversation, nodding your head appropriately, but unable to get yourself back in it and fearful that you will be found out?

2. Did you spend a lot of time in fantasy as a child, so much so that teachers or parents criticized you for being "in another world" a good bit of the time?

3. Does fantasy interfere with your life as an adult? Do you daydream about pleasant things so much that it jeopardizes your job or compromises your relationships?

4. Do you feel like quite a different person from time to time?

5. Do friends suggest that you seem quite changeable, different from day to day?

6. Are you accident-prone?

7. Do you make a lot of "Freudian slips" — where you think one thing but say or write something quite different, even the opposite?

8. Do you have a sense that part of you is missing or had to be jettisoned along the way?

9. Do you notice things about your sex life that you think

are weird, like hating to be touched in ways that most people seem to enjoy?

10. Do you have large chunks of your childhood that are devoid of memories?

11. Are you more indecisive than most of the people you know?

[A score of six or more "yes" answers is suggestive of Ego State Disorder.]

CAUTION: This is not a standardized test, and the scoring is *only* suggestive.

BIBLIOGRAPHY

Csikszentmihalyi, Mihaly. *Flow: The Psychology Of Optimal Experience.* New York: Harper & Row, 1990.

Federn, P. *Ego Psychology And The Psychoses.* New York: Basic Books, 1952.

Hilgard, Ernest R. *Divided Consciousness.* New York: John Wiley & Sons, 1986.

Janet, P. *The Major Symptoms Of Hysteria.* New York: Macmillan, 1907.

Kafka, Franz. *Erzahlungen,* 3rd ed. New York: Schocken Books, 1946.

Orne, M. T. "The Simulation of Hypnosis: Why, How, and What It Means." *International Journal of Clinical and Experimental Hypnosis,* 19 (1971), pp. 183-210.

Pitblado, Colin, and Judianne Dense-Gerber. "Pattern-evoked Potential Differences among the Personalities of a Multiple: Some New Phenomena." Paper presented at the Third Annual Conference on Multiple Personality, Chicago, IL, Sept. 18-21, 1986.

Prince, M. *The Dissociation Of A Personality.* New York: Longmans Green, 1906.

Putnam, Frank W., M.D. *Diagnosis And Treatment Of Multiple Personality Disorder.* New York: The Guilford Press, 1989.

Schiller, Friedrich. *Die Rauber,* Vol. 3, *Schiller's Werke,* ed. Herbert Stubenrauch. Weimar: H. Bohlaus Nachfolger, 1953.

Schultz, Duane. *Theories Of Personality.* Belmont, CA: Brooks/Cole, 1990.

Solzhenitsyn, A. I. *The Gulag Archipelago,* 1918-1956. New York: Harper & Row, 1973.

Waldeck, Peter B. *The Split Self From Goethe To Broch.* Bucknell Univ. Press, 1979.

Watkins, John. "The Bianchi Case: Sociopath or Multiple Personality?" *International Journal of Clinical and Experimental Hypnosis,* 32 (1984), pp. 67-101.

ABOUT THE AUTHOR

Alan G. Marshall, Ph.D., is a practicing psychothera-
pist. He is a graduate of Cornell University with a B.A.
degree in Philosophy and Psychology, and he has an M.A.
and Ph.D. in Clinical Psychology, both from Vanderbilt
University. His papers and publications include: *The Effect
of Two Anxiety Manipulations on Short-term Memory* (with
R. Blanton), 1967; *Psychotics See Themselves on Videotape,*
1968; *Depression as a Pattern of Emotions and Feelings*
(with C. E. Izaard), New York Academic Press, 1973; and
"Cerebral Electrotherapeutic Treatment of Depression,"
Journal of Consulting and Clinical Psychology, Vol. 28 (1972),
pp. 71-75.

Dr. Marshall is married and has two sons. He lives in
Asheville, North Carolina, where he continues to write on
subjects of interest to his profession and to the lay person,
including a semifictional autobiography of an Ego State.

PEOPLE IN PIECES:
Multiple Personality In Milder Forms
& Greater Numbers

For additional copies of *People In Pieces,* telephone TOLL FREE 1-800-356-9315 or FAX TOLL FREE 1-800-242-0046. MasterCard/ VISA accepted.

To order *People In Pieces* directly from the publisher, send your check or money order for $12.95 plus $3.00 shipping and handling $15.95 postpaid) to: Rainbow Books, Inc., Order Dept. 1-T, P.O. Box 430, Highland City, FL 33846-0430.

For QUANTITY PURCHASES, telephone Rainbow Books, Inc., (813) 648-4420 or write to Rainbow Books, Inc., P.O. Box 430, Highland City, FL 33846-0430.